Preaching the Just Word

WALTER J. BURGHARDT, S.J.

Preaching the Just Word

Yale University Press / New Haven and London

Designed by Nancy Ovedovitz and set in Simoncini Garamond type by Tseng Information Systems, Inc. Printed in the United States of America by Vail-Ballou Press, Binghamton, New York.

Library of Congress Cataloging-in-Publication Data
Burghardt, Walter J.
Preaching the just word / Walter J. Burghardt.
p. cm.
Includes bibliographical references (p.) and index.
ISBN 0-300-06768-2 (cloth . alk. paper)
1. Christianity and justice—Catholic Church.   2. Catholic preaching.   3. Catholic Church—Doctrines.   I. Title.
BX1795.J87B87   1996
261.8—dc20   96-15779
CIP

A catalogue record for this book is available from the British Library.
The paper in this book meets the guidelines for permanence and durability of the Committee on Production Guidelines for Book Longevity of the Council on Library Resources.

10   9   8   7   6   5   4   3   2   1

Contents

Preface

The invitation from the Yale Divinity School to present the 1994 Lyman Beecher Lectures on Preaching reached me as a delightful surprise. A surprise because the long history of these lectures reveals a succession of preacher/presenters that is not only impressive but daunting indeed. Delightful, nevertheless, because I was able to respond immediately to Dean Thomas W. Ogletree with a firm yes. A word on the series, then a word on my subject.

The Lyman Beecher Lectureship on Preaching was established at Yale Divinity on April 12, 1871, in memory of Lyman Beecher (1775-1863), a Presbyterian and Congregationalist minister who held pastorates in East Hampton, New York; Litchfield, Connecticut; and Boston. In harmony with the wishes of the donor, businessman Henry W. Sage, the lectureship was to be filled from time to time, upon appointment of the Yale Corporation, by a minister of the gospel, of any evangelical denomination, who has been markedly successful in the special work of the Christian ministry. With the authorization of the donor, the Corporation voted in May 1882 "that henceforth the Lyman Beecher lecturer shall be invited to lecture on a branch of pastoral theology or in any other topic appropriate to the work of the Christian ministry." In December 1893 the donor authorized the Corporation, "if at any time they should deem it desirable to do so, to appoint a layman instead of a minister to deliver the course of lectures on the Lyman Beecher Foundation."[1]

Beecher lecturers have included such prestigious preachers as Henry Ward Beecher, Phillips Brooks, Henry Van Dyke, Charles D. Williams, Harry Emerson Fosdick, W. R. Inge, George A. Buttrick, Ralph W. Sockman, Reinhold Niebuhr, Henry Knox Sherrill, Angus Dun, Douglas Horton, Joseph Sittler, James Edward Lesslie Newbigin, Sidney Mead, Paul Pruyser, Paul Ramsey, Ivan Illich, David H. C. Read, Frederick Buechner, Fred B. Craddock, William Sloane Coffin, Sydney E. Ahlstrom, Phyllis Trible, Krister Stendahl, James Forbes, Walter Brueggemann, Brevard Childs, Margaret Farley, and Leander Keck.

My choice of a general subject, "The Christian Pulpit and the Just Word," stemmed in large measure from recent preoccupations. In the spring of 1990, I was faced with a significant transition in my life. For thirty-two years I had taught, lectured, and published in the area of my theological predilection, the Fathers of the Church, or, more generally, the early Christian writers down to the seventh or eighth century. For forty-four years I had been, successively, managing editor and editor-in-chief of the journal *Theological Studies*. All my priestly life, an unabashed lover of words and the Word, I had engaged in the art and craft of preaching — with an increasing concern in the 1980s for the poor and the oppressed, the disregarded and the marginalized.

Now I was confronted with an unprecedented need: to leave strictly scholarly pursuits in an academic environment, to leave the journal in younger hands, and to focus on some single type of Christian and ministerial activity that might engage my predominant background and talents. Background? Theology. Talents? Communication: preaching, lecturing, writing.

I was then a senior member of the Woodstock Theological Center, a nonprofit research institute established in 1974 by the Maryland and New York Provinces of the Society of Jesus to address topics of social, economic, and political importance from a theological and ethical perspective.

The Center proved to be the seed plot of my dream. Located at George-town University in the District of Columbia, the institute offers research, forums, and publications on such issues as human rights, business ethics, the environment, and public philosophy. But indispensable though they are, publications and forums reach only a small proportion of our Catholic people. How could we expand the Center's influence, stimulate American Catholicism *as a whole* to live and spread the Church's social gospel?

An obvious question: where do Catholics gather regularly—hardly a majority but consistently in incomparable numbers—week after week, year after year? At the weekend liturgies: to listen to the Word in the context of worship. Millions of potential listeners, a captive audience that a TV network might understandably envy. The obvious approach to my gathering dream: preaching.

But the dream had a nightmarish aura. Catholic preaching, for all its upsurge since the Second Vatican Council (1962-65), is not our most successful ministry. At times I resonate to the observation of the president of the University of Rochester, Dennis O'Brien, that on Monday morning most people at the train station would likely appraise church service as "Saturday Night Live, Sunday Morning Deadly."[2] The problem is compounded when impoverished preaching has for content what is known as "social justice." For a constant reaction to such preaching has been the closing of Catholic ears, even indignation and anger at the suggestion that hard-earned money should be rerouted to wastrels on relief. Easy enough for you, dear preacher, to preach about the poor, to rhapsodize about the less fortunate; we have to live with them, and we know what most of them are really like.

If our sermons are to revive the social gospel, if our homilies are to inspire as well as inform, our preachers must be set aflame. Not just provided with information, data, skills, strategies, important as these are. Even more importantly, a spirituality; in fact, a conversion that turns the preacher inside out, puts "fire in the belly." Hence my project Preaching the Just Word, an effort to improve significantly the preaching of justice issues, primarily in the Catholic pulpits of the country, gradually on a broader, ecumenical level.

The method? Retreat/workshops, a week in length—the Spiritual Exercises of St. Ignatius Loyola in the context of social justice, led by teams of five or six, experts in biblical justice, the Church's tradition, effective preaching, profound spirituality, today's culture, and the liturgy. Not to solve complex issues in a sermon. Rather, to raise consciousness, stimulate awareness. Through persuasive homilies draw people of the parish together to mull over three questions: (1) What are the problem areas in our parish? (2) What resources do we command to address these issues? (3) How shall we turn theory to practice?

It is in this context that I decided to focus my Beecher Lectures on the Christian pulpit and social justice. The occasion promised an attractive opportunity to put together three primary facets of the problem in question: biblical justice, the Christian tradition, and the cry of the poor. Biblical justice, because ethical justice, for all its significance, does not do justice to the Jewish and Christian challenge. The Christian tradition, because the extensive, profound social teaching of Christianity may well be the Church's best-kept secret. The cry of the poor, because social doctrine, however deep, remains at best a head trip unless it is touched to, in fact stems in large measure from, the less fortunate images of Jesus, those who share far more of his crucifixion than of his resurrection. And all this with a special concern for the preacher; for "faith comes from what is heard, and what is heard comes through Christ's message" (Rom 10:17).

At the request of the gracious publishers, the original lectures have been significantly expanded. Understandably so, for each of the actual lectures had to be compressed into an hour's time. This extended version, while retaining all of the oral presentation, has permitted me to probe problems more extensively and to grapple with a number of new but related issues. The result is, I believe, a proper book that is more likely to engage the attention of scholars as well as a broadly educated public. Such attention is critical not only to me personally but for the social gospel itself. For I raise questions, assemble arguments, and propose answers that lay no claim to infallibility, yet are highly pertinent for social justice theory, for effective preaching, and, even more urgently, for life-and-death struggles of men, women, and children across the world.

Preaching the Just Word in Scripture

Several years ago, the creative Scripture scholar Walter Brueggemann addressed what he called the problem of "scandal" in the preaching of social, political, and economic issues:

> In Luke 7, after John the Baptist raises his christological question through his disciples whether Jesus is the Christ, and after Jesus answers with specificity that "the blind see, the lame walk, lepers are cleansed, the dead are raised, and the poor rejoice," Jesus adds, "blessed is the one who is not scandalized by me" (v. 23). Or as I have rendered it, "lucky are you, if you are not upset." The theological scandal of biblical faith, especially when rendered into political, economic issues, is indeed upsetting.
>
> How is a pastor to give voice to this scandal in a society that is hostile to it, in a church that is often unwilling to host the scandal, and when we ourselves as teachers and pastors of the church are somewhat queasy about the scandal as it touches our own lives? How can the radical dimension of the Bible as it touches public reality be heard in the church?[1]

Two primary questions dominate this first presentation of mine: (1) What precisely is this "radical dimension of the Bible" that gives rise to "scandal" in the Church? (2) How might we proclaim this radical Scripture effectively, despite the "scandal" among Christians?

Biblical Justice

My first question: What precisely is this "radical dimension of the Bible" that gives rise to "scandal" in the Church? It centers on the word *justice*. But what should justice mean in a Christian context? About seven years ago, the Jesuit social scientist Philip Land opened an encyclopedia article on justice with a quotation from the Hebrew prophet Amos: "Let justice roll down like waters" (Amos 5:24). Land continued:

> Prior to Vatican II no Roman Catholic treatise on justice would have begun with scripture. It would have taken its start from the [ethical] definition of justice—*Suum cuique tradere*—to render to each [what is] one's due and proceeded then to analyze in the light of reason the various relations this involves. With Vatican II but especially with the 1971 Synod, Justice in the World, justice becomes a call to the Christian from the God of the two Testaments.[2]

The crucial point is this: When Micah declared to Israel, "What does the Lord require of you but to do justice?" (Mic 6:8), he was not imposing on God's people simply or primarily an ethical construct: Give to each man, woman, and child what is due to each, what each person has a strict right to demand, because he or she is a human being, has rights that can be proven by philosophy or have been written into law. What, then, was the justice God wanted to "roll down like waters"? In one sense the biblical concept of justice is too rich, too opulent, to imprison in a definition. Back in 1977 the biblical scholar John R. Donahue shaped a working definition with admirable succinctness:

> In general terms the biblical idea of justice can be described as *fidelity to the demands of a relationship.* In contrast to modern individualism the Israelite is in a world where "to live" is to be united with others in a social context either by bonds of family or by covenant relationships. This web of relationships—king with people, judge with complainants, family with tribe and kinfolk, the community with the resident alien and suffering in their midst and all with the covenant God—constitutes the world in which life is played out.[3]

Within this context, in what sense is God just? Because God always acts as God should, is invariably faithful to God's promises, for example, defending or vindicating God's people, punishing violations of the covenant, never forgetting a forgetful people. When are people just? When they are in right relationship to their God, to their sisters and brothers, to the whole of created reality. When God declared all of creation "very good" (Gen 1:31), it was because simply everything was in right order, in proper relation: humanity (*adam*) to God, humans among themselves, humans and nonhuman reality toward one another. Justice has to do with the right ordering of all relationships, and so it is central to all of human living.[4]

Put simply, justice was a whole network of relationships; and the profound basis of these relationships was Israel's covenant with God. The Israelites were to father the fatherless and mother the motherless, were to welcome the stranger, feed the sojourner, show hospitality to the resident alien, not because the orphan and the outsider deserved it, but because this was the way God had acted with Israel. A text in Deuteronomy is telling: "Love the sojourner (the stranger, the resident alien), for you were sojourners in the land of Egypt" (Deut 10:19). In freeing the oppressed, they were mirroring the loving God who had delivered *them* from oppression, had freed them from Pharaoh.

Another way of phrasing it: justice, for the Jew, was not a question simply, or even primarily, of human deserving, of human law. The Jews were to give to others what they themselves had been given by God, were to act toward one another and toward the stranger as God had acted toward Israel — and *precisely because* God had acted this way. Their justice was to image not the justice of man and woman but the justice of Yahweh. For Israel, the practice of justice thus understood was an expression of steadfast love — God's love and their own. Not to execute justice was not to worship God.

Fidelity to relationships. For an Israelite, to be just was to be in right relation in all the aspects of one's life, properly postured not only toward God but toward other men and women within the community. And indeed there is at least a basis in Scripture for justice as right relation toward all of God's creation: the "earth" (Gen 1:28) that calls not for despotic abuse but for reverential care; the "crops" that the rich man in Jesus' parable (Lk 12:14-21) is to "guard against all kinds of greed"; the "creation" that Paul claims is yearning to be "set free from its bondage to decay," to "obtain the freedom of the glory of the children of God" (Rom 8:21).

At this point I suggest that an even broader context is imperative. For a perilous proposition pervades a large segment of American Catholicism, perhaps much of our American Christian culture. It asserts that Christianity, by its very nature, is concerned exclusively with the relation of the soul to eternity, that the essential realization religion should provide is the worthlessness of human expectations of a better life on earth. It insists that the Son of God took our flesh not to relieve our suffering but to forgive our sins, and so the Church's function is to focus not on violations of social justice but on the undying hardness of human hearts.

Social Focus of Scripture

The thesis does violence to Scripture. Those who read in the sacred text a sheerly personal, individualistic morality have not understood the Torah, have not sung the Psalms, have not been burned by the prophets, have not perceived the implications and the very burden of Jesus' message, and must inevitably play fast and loose with St. Paul.

The social focus of God's Book is evident on the first page; the song of creation is its overture. Our incredibly imaginative God did not have in mind isolated units, autonomous entities, scattered disparately around a globe, basically independent each of every other—entities that might one day decide through a social contract to join together for self-aggrandizement, huddle together for self-protection. God had in mind a people, a human family, a community of persons, a body genuinely one. Moreover, it is not exploitation that the Hebrew word for "have dominion" (Gen 1:26) mandates, but reverential care for God's creation. John Donahue has summed up the significance of the creation stories in two powerful sentences: "Men and women are God's representatives and conversation partners in the world, with a fundamental dignity that must be respected and fostered. They are to exist in interdependence and mutual support and are to care for the world with respect, as for a gift received from God." [5]

It is this divine dream for human living that the Second Vatican Council stated unambiguously: "God . . . has willed that all men and women should constitute one family." Again, "God did not create man and woman for life in isolation, but for the formation of social unity." And "this solidarity must be constantly increased until that day on which it will be brought to perfection. Then, saved by grace, men and women will offer flawless glory to God as a family beloved of God and of Christ their brother."[6]

This divine idea began to take concrete shape when God, bringing an oppressed mass out of Egypt, created a *people* which was to gather in prayer and thanksgiving (cult) and to live according to God's constitution *(torah).*[7] Why this particular body of men and women? Moses' words to God's people as recorded in Deuteronomy are splendidly pertinent here:

> It was not because you were more numerous than any other people that the Lord set His heart on you and chose you—for you were the fewest of all peoples. It was because the Lord loved you and kept the oath that He swore to your ancestors, that the Lord has brought you out with a mighty hand, and redeemed you from the house of slavery, from the hand of Pharaoh, king of Egypt. (Deut 7:7-8)

Those who were no people God made into a people. The Exodus, therefore, was not simply a liberation from slavery; it was the formation of a new social order—"a contrast society," in Norbert Lohfink's pungent expression.[8] As Donahue put it, "While liberation from oppression is a fundamental aspect of the Exodus narrative, it is not simply *freedom from* which is important, but *freedom for* the formation of a community which lives under the covenant."[9] God summoned the entire community to response and responsibility. Remember how Moses charged the Israelites:

> When your children ask you in time to come, "What is the meaning of the decrees and the statutes and the ordinances that the Lord our God has commanded you?" then you shall say to your children: "We were Pharaoh's slaves in Egypt, but the Lord brought us out of Egypt with a mighty hand. The Lord displayed before our eyes great and awesome signs and wonders against Egypt, against Pharaoh and all his household. He brought us out of there in order to bring us in, to give us the land that He promised on oath to our ancestors. Then the Lord commanded us to observe all these statutes, to fear the Lord our God, for our lasting good, so as to keep us alive, as is now the case. If we diligently observe this entire commandment before the Lord our God, as He has commanded us, we will be in the right." (Deut 6:20-25)

This covenant between God and a people was a symbol of proper relationships—to God and among men and women. What did the covenant demand? "You shall love the Lord your God with all your heart, all your soul, all your might" (Deut 6:5). And "you shall love your neighbor as yourself" (Lev 19:18). The people of God is radically social. What did this involve in the concrete?

The Scripture scholar Carolyn Osiek, in one of our Preaching the Just Word retreat/workshops, revealed concretely how the Israelite relationships that flowed from common identity as members of the covenant community can be seen through four concerns:

1. *Trustworthiness.* What Yahweh desires is "steadfast love" rather than sheer sacrifice (Hos 6:6). What does the Lord require of Israel? "Do justice *(mišpāṭ),* love kindness *(ḥesed),* and walk humbly with your God" (Mic 6:8). Particularly prohibited is partiality in lawsuits, even partiality toward the poor (Exod 23:3; Lev 19:15). This does not contradict the special consideration that the powerful are to provide the poor and defenseless.

2. *Relationships between rich and poor.* Save in legal contexts, justice is not *equal* treatment; justice is *appropriate* treatment that will equalize the relationship and provide access to resources. Examples are vivid. When grain, grapes, or olives are harvested, the reaper is not to return to pick up what was missed the first time. These "leftovers" must go to the poor, to the widow and orphan, to the resident alien (Lev 19:9-10; Deut 24:19-22). Interest must not be taken on a loan (Exod 22:25; Lev 25:35-37; Deut 23:20-21).[10] A cloak taken in pledge from a poor person must be returned before nightfall, "for that is his only covering, it is his mantle for his body; in what else shall he sleep?" (Exod 22:26-27). Abuses of such sensitive relationships provoke outraged outcries from the prophets:

> The Lord enters into judgment
>   with the elders and princes of His people:
> "It is you who have devoured the vineyard,
>   the spoil of the poor is in your houses.
> What do you mean by crushing my people,
>   by grinding the face of the poor?" (Isa 3:14-15)

3. *Relationships between male and female.* In the patriarchal society that was Israel, women ranked among the defenseless who had to be protected, first by the powerful males of their own family, but also by the powerful of the society. In consequence, we find legislation for the rights of a girl sold

into slavery by her parents—protective indeed, but hardly consonant with the dignity today's Jew or Christian would demand for a daughter of God (Exod 21:7-11). There is legislation for the rights of a rape victim (Exod 22: 16-17), for the rights of a widow (vv. 22-24). New in Deuteronomy is protection of a wife's reputation against slander (22:13-19) and the rights of a female captive (21:10-14).

4. *Relationships between citizen and stranger,* or resident alien. Here it is not a question of hospitality, which is directed by different rules; here it is treatment of non-Israelites living in Israelite territory: "You shall not oppress a resident alien; you know the heart of an alien [you know how an alien feels], for you were aliens in the land of Egypt" (Exod 23:9; see 22:21). More than not oppressing, "you shall also love the stranger, for you were strangers in the land of Egypt" (Deut 10:19; see 24:17). What lies behind such ordinances? The land actually is God's; all humans, even Israelites, are aliens. "The land is mine; with me you are but aliens and tenants" (Deut 25:23).

Even though all this is guaranteed by law, behind the law lies the covenant, "the great God, mighty and awesome, who is not partial and takes no bribe, who executes justice for the orphan and the widow, and who loves the strangers, providing them food and clothing" (Deut 10:17-18). Behind it is the Lord who dealt thus with Israel when the people were aliens, strangers, in Egypt (v. 19). The rights do not stem primarily from the law; for the law itself is an effort to express what the covenant demands in actual living.

The covenant relationship explains why concern for the poor and the marginal is pervasive in the Hebrew Bible. Take the prophets. Through Isaiah and Hosea, through Amos and Micah and Jeremiah, Yahweh ceaselessly proclaims to Israel that the Lord rejects precisely those things the Israelites think will make God happy. Yahweh is weary of burnt offerings, delights not in the blood of bulls or lambs, finds incense an abomination, hates their appointed feasts, will not listen to their prayers and to the melody of their harps, does not want rivers of oil, thousands of rams, even their firstborn. Why not? Not because these are unacceptable in themselves; rather because two essential ingredients are missing: steadfast love and justice.[11] One passage from Isaiah says it all in powerful rhetoric:

Is not this the fast that I choose:
  to loose the bonds of injustice,
  to undo the thongs of the yoke,
to let the oppressed go free,
  and to break every yoke?
Is it not to share your bread with the hungry,
  and bring the homeless poor into your house;
when you see the naked, to cover them,
  and not to hide yourself from your own flesh?
Then your light shall break forth like the dawn,
  and your healing shall spring up quickly;
your vindicator [vindication?] shall go before you,
  the glory of the Lord shall be your rear guard.
Then you shall call, and the Lord will answer;
  you shall cry for help, and He will say, Here I am. (Isa 58:6–9a)

It is precisely this fashioning of a people, this call to community, that gives sin its most significant characteristic. In Scripture, sin involves not only our traditional "offense against God" but also the sundering of community. The whole of Scripture from Genesis to Revelation is the story of struggle for community, of lapses into disintegration, division, enmity. If biblical justice is "fidelity to the demands of a relationship," then sin is a refusal of responsibility; sin creates division, alienation, dissension, marginalization, rejection; sin dis-members the body.

Scripture's story of salvation time and again confirms the growing conviction in our time that there is no such thing as a sheerly "private" sin or a sin confined to "two consenting adults." All sin is social, just as all grace and goodness is social. I see this most vividly when I read the novelist/preacher Frederick Buechner comparing humanity to an enormous spider web:

If you touch it anywhere, you set the whole thing trembling. . . . As we move around this world and as we act with kindness, perhaps, or with indifference, or with hostility, toward the people we meet, we too are setting the great spider web a-tremble. The life that I touch for good or ill will touch another life, and that in turn another, until who knows where the trembling stops or in what far place and time my touch will be felt. Our lives are linked. No man is an island.[12]

It is the Israelite tradition on justice that sparked the ministry of Jesus. It was summed up in the synagogue at Nazareth, in what Luke presents as

Jesus' programmatic presentation: "The Spirit of the Lord is upon me, for [the Lord] has anointed me, has sent me to preach good news to the poor, to proclaim release for prisoners and sight for the blind, to send the downtrodden away relieved" (Lk 4:18; cf. Isa 61:1-2).[13] Matthew had already grasped this, for he applied to Jesus the prophecy in Isaiah: "I will put my Spirit upon him, and he will proclaim justice to the Gentiles. . . . He will not break a bruised reed or quench a smoldering wick until he brings justice to victory" (Mt 12:18-20; cf. Isa 42:1-4). In harmony with Hosea, he wants not sacrifice but compassion, mercy (cf. Mt 12:7, 23:23).

For Jesus, too, the just man or woman is not primarily someone who gives to another what that other *deserves.* Jesus inaugurates a new covenant, where the most significant relationship is the monosyllable that says it all: love—and astonishingly, where loving one's neighbor, already commanded in Leviticus (19:18), is said by Jesus to be "like" loving God (Mt 22:39). "Love your neighbor as yourself" is not a psychological balancing act: as much or as little as you love yourself, that much love or that little love shower on your neighbor. It means I am to love my neighbor as if he or she were another "I," as if I were in my neighbor's place, as if I were standing in his or her shoes. This is what our covenant demands—what Jesus summed up when he said, "Love one another as I have loved you" (Jn 15:12).

Not an invitation; a command. Not to give in proportion to merit, but to love as Jesus loved. Not a *quid pro quo,* but a self-giving over and above the demands of sheerly human ethics. This is New Testament justice: love as Jesus loved. The kind of love that impelled God's unique Son to wear our flesh; to be born of a woman as we are born; to thirst and tire as we do; to respond with compassion to a hungry crowd, the bereavement of a mother, the fever of Peter's mother-in-law, the sorrow of a sinful woman; to weep over a dead friend and a hostile city; to spend himself especially for the bedeviled and bewildered, the poverty-stricken and the marginalized; to die in exquisite agony so that others might live.

The Scripture scholar Sarah Ann Sharkey has suggested that, to appreciate justice in Jesus, we should read Mark's Gospel in its entirety, carefully watching Jesus, his disciples, and other characters, particularly the "little" people.[14] Without speaking specifically of justice, Mark is constantly dealing with the idea, with the reality of making all relationships right. Especially impressive is his stress on the cost of engaging in the ministry of justice: the cross.

There is Peter's fevered mother-in-law and the woman hemorrhaging for twelve years, the man with a withered hand and the paralyzed man let down through the roof. There is the ostracized leper and Levi the tax collector. There is the convulsed boy foaming at the mouth and the man emerging from the tombs with an unclean spirit. There is the living child Jesus took in his arms and the dead twelve-year-old daughter of a synagogue leader he said was only sleeping. There is the blind beggar Bartimaeus and the thousands who sat close to Jesus for three days with nothing to eat. There is the man who yearned for eternal life but was terribly attached to his own possessions, and the poor widow who put her last penny in the treasury. There are those closest of friends, his special disciples, who could be unbelievably dense when he taught them, who slept while he agonized in the garden, who deserted him when his hour had come. There are those grouped together as simply "sinners." All these Jesus moved in different ways to right relationships.

"Jesus," observes Carolyn Osiek, "is a son of the covenant; his approach to justice is through observance of the law as response to the covenant."[15] The four community relationships highlighted in Osiek's treatment of the Israelite tradition are matched in the "Jesus movement": (1) Jesus demanded that his disciples be *trustworthy,* reliable servants waiting for their master's return (Mt 24:42-51; Lk 12:35-48), even if they had to confess themselves "unprofitable, worthless, useless" (Lk 17:10). (2) Jesus came from the peasant class and represented a *peasant perspective* in an agrarian society. While exposing the wealthy and the powerful, he also pointed an accusatory finger at the underclass, for example, the unjust slave forgiven a huge debt by his master, yet refusing to have patience with a fellow slave's much smaller debt (Mt 18:23-35). Moreover, Luke's harsh critique of wealth raises the question whether in his mind wealth is compatible with Christianity (e.g., Lk 6:24). (3) Always respectful of *women,* Jesus related to them at times in ways unacceptable to the culture and prejudicial to his reputation: healing a bent woman on the Sabbath (Lk 13:10-17); permitting a "sinner" (Lk 7:36-50) and an unclean (hemorrhaging) woman to touch him (Mt 9:20-22; Mk 5:25-34; Lk 8:43-48); attending a private dinner with two women friends, Martha and Mary (Lk 10:38-42); speaking to a female stranger in public, and she a Samaritan (Jn 4:1-42). (4) As for the *stranger*, the outsider, Jesus was uncommonly open to Gentiles, even felt comfortable in their territory, on their turf (especially in Mark). And there are the striking Matthean "bookends," the astrologers from the East (2:1-12) and the commissioning of the Eleven to "make disciples of all nations" (28:16-20).

Such was, in large measure, the profound approach of the early Church, envisioning itself as the covenant community of the baptized—the Body of Christ, branches abiding in the vine, disciples committed to loving all others "as I have loved you" (Jn 15:12):

1. To be trustworthy was essential to Christian living; for "as surely as God is faithful," as surely as in Jesus "every one of God's promises is a yes," so through Jesus the disciple is always ready to respond with a yes, an amen "to the glory of God" (2 Cor 1:18-20). In fact, Ananias and Sapphira lost their lives not because they kept from the community some of the proceeds from the sale of their property, but because they had lied to the Holy Spirit and to the community (Acts 5:1-11).

2. The Letter of James (2:1-9) protests "partiality," "favoritism" shown to the rich when Christians assemble—for example, priority seating. It contradicts genuine belief in the Lord Jesus; it is failing to love our neighbors as other selves; it is sinful. Nor can faith save if it is divorced from deeds, specifically failure to "supply the bodily needs" of the hungry and the naked (2:14-17).

3. As for male-female relationships, we have what Osiek calls "ambiguous new beginnings in a patriarchal society in which male and female were not understood to be equal." The holiness of baptized women, specifically the sanctifying influence of a believing wife, is recognized by Paul (1 Cor 7:12-16). Women such as Phoebe and Prisca (Priscilla) play an active role in Christian ministry (Rom 16:1-5). For Mark, Luke, and John, women are the first to witness and proclaim Jesus' resurrection (Mk 16:9-10; Lk 24:1-12; Jn 20:17-18)—so prominently that in one striking tradition Mary Magdalene has been termed "apostle to the apostles." [16] A Samaritan woman of dubious reputation "has a real missionary function," "has sown the seed and thus prepared for the apostolic harvest" (Jn 4). [17] Still, as Osiek has pointed out, the traditional restrictions on women in the assembly, marriage, and public life remain (1 Cor 14:34-35; 1 Tim 2:11-15; 1 Pet 3:1-7).

4. As for the stranger, the alien, the unbeliever, the evildoer, there is a recurrent tension between the holy community and openness to "the world." Examples abound. Certain evildoers are to be avoided, but to avoid all "you would then need to go out of the world" (1 Cor 5:9-13). It would seem that Christian prayer services were open to outsiders (1 Cor 14:16) but not the Lord's Supper. An unbeliever's invitation to a meal need not be refused, unless scandal is involved, for example, food "offered in sacrifice" (1 Cor 10:23-30). The once alien Gentiles are now "citizens with the saints and also members of the household of God" (Eph 2:11-22), while Christians are actually "aliens and exiles" in the world, with their citizenship in heaven (1 Pet 1:17, 2:11).[18]

The response of the early Christian communities to the "new commandment" of Jesus is summed up, in a sense, in Matthew's presentation of the Last Judgment (25:31-46). If *anyone* is hungry or thirsty, naked or a stranger, sick or in prison, it is always Christ who clamors for bread or water, Christ who cries to be clothed or welcomed, Christ whom you visit on a bed of pain or behind bars.[19] And the First Letter of John is terribly uncompromising: "If anyone has the world's goods and sees his brother in need, yet closes his heart against him, how does God's love abide in him?" (1 Jn 3:17). Here is a vision of community where, as Paul puts it, no one, absolutely no one, can say to any other, "I have no need of you" (1 Cor 12:12 ff.). Not the rich to the poor, not the powerful to the powerless, not the bold and beautiful to the timid and repulsive. For we are to be one as Jesus and his Father are one (cf. Jn 17:20-23).

The Earth

Very simply, a covenant people is a people involved not only with God but with people, not only with the Other but with all the others. It is St. Paul's injunction, "Bear one another's burdens, and in this way you will fulfill the law of Christ" (Gal 6:2). But it is not only God and people that lay demands on our covenant fidelity, that challenge our responsibility. A mute but agonizing cry for justice leaps from the rest of God's creation—what I embrace in the word *earth*. I mean all that is not God or the human person.

During January and February 1974, in the context of Paul VI's proclamation of a Holy Year of grace, with the theme "Renewal and Reconciliation," I gave six addresses on the NBC radio program *Guideline*. The addresses were published the same year in a booklet entitled *Towards Reconciliation*.[20] Four chapters dealt successively with rupture and reconciliation (1) between humans and God, (2) within the human person, (3) among humans, and (4) between humans and nature.

Reflecting on our relations with nature, I recalled an interview by a New York newspaper with the social philosopher and psychoanalyst Erich Fromm.[21] Fromm had come to this country in the early 1930s, an exile from Hitler's Germany, his hopes high for life and work in a vibrant America. Forty years later he felt profound fear for his adopted country. "The United States is not yet entirely in hell. There is a very small chance of avoiding it, but I am not an optimist."

Why such gloom? One reason was our "unrestrained industrialism." As Fromm saw it, after the Second World War, America's industrial machine spewed an endless flow of motorcars and pleasure boats, refrigerators and air conditioners, barbecue pits and heated swimming pools. Such incredible excess of material things, Fromm claimed—the machine process—has minified man and woman, made our own lives seem unimportant to us. "We have grown soft from it at a sacrifice of, what shall I call it, the soul." And, on the whole, we "have accepted the logic of machinery, which is to demonstrate how machinery works. The ultimate purpose of making a gun is to use it." In consequence, Fromm concluded, "America has become the world's most destructive society." Not only had we bombed Vietnam back to the Bronze Age. "Our society is also internally destructive. In the last decade or so, a million people have been killed in highway accidents. We produce cars with built-in obsolescence. Knowing the possible dangers, we continue to pollute the environment. And we subsidize violence on the screen—movies in which human life is depicted as brutish and cheap."

Since Fromm's jeremiad, the destruction has hardly diminished. As America turned into the 1990s, continuous chemical emissions from one hundred million refrigerators, ninety million air conditioners, and one hundred thousand central air conditioning units in large buildings were the major causes for the depletion of the world's ozone layer—a critical factor for cancer.[22] Twenty-three million tons of chemicals were being released annually by industry and automobiles, causing surface-level ozone and smog that result in lung irritation.[23] According to the Department of Energy, hundreds of thousands of Americans working in or living near nuclear weapons plants or testing facilities had been directly exposed to radioactivity either through accidents or during normal operations.[24] Having increased the carbon dioxide in the air by about 25% in the last century, and having doubled the level of methane, we have substantially altered the earth's atmosphere.[25]

As I write these lines, I read that poaching in nearly half of our country's 366 park areas has reached unprecedented proportions. "The illegal killing of animals is a $200 million-a-year business." Brown bears and bighorn sheep, elk and king snakes, ducks and spiders and butterflies—nothing is safe. Perhaps three thousand black bears are taken illegally each year. The sites designated for wildlife's preservation "are becoming an abattoir, almost as if someone had let a serial killer into Noah's ark." [26]

What I found frightening in Fromm's time, what continues to frighten me, is that we seem to be enlarging the enmity that exists between humans and our earth. It is as if we began with God's malediction in Genesis, "Cursed is the ground because of you" (Gen 3:17), experienced how reluctant nature often is to serve us, vowed that with our know-how and our power we rational creatures would enslave the irrational, and then carried our vow relentlessly to its logical conclusion. We have conquered the earth; it is subject, or soon will be, to our every will and whim. Only . . . the slave has turned on its master; cold reason is no longer in control; out of the nonhuman we have fashioned a monster, and the monster threatens to strangle us. Little wonder that in 1992 the Union of Concerned Scientists issued a declaration over 1,575 signatures that said in part: "Human beings and the natural world are on a collision course. Many of our current practices put at serious risk the future that we wish for human society and the plant and animal kingdoms, and may so alter the living world that it will be unable to sustain life in the manner that we know." [27]

What has this to do with Scripture? Some critics blame our ecological crisis on the Christian understanding of the Hebrew Testament. As they see it, the scientific stance of the Western world goes back to the first chapter of the Bible (Gen 1:27–28):

God created humankind in God's image, in the image of God God created humankind; male and female God created them. God blessed them, and God said to them: "Be fruitful and multiply, and fill the earth and subdue it; and have dominion over the fish of the sea and over the birds of the air and over every living thing that moves upon the earth."

Subdue . . . have dominion. Christianity (so the charge runs) sees in humankind the one center of the universe. All else—soil and sea and sky, blue marlin or bird of paradise, oil or coal or natural gas—all that is not man or woman has for purpose, for destiny, to serve humans, to serve their purpose, to serve their pleasure.

And (so the charge continues) Western man and Western woman have lived their theology, played their role of master and mistress, with a vengeance. In laboratory and forest, in factory and refectory, we pillage and we rape, we devour and we waste. Why not? It is I who am God's image, master actually or potentially of all I survey—king of the earth (said some early Christian writers) as God is King of the universe. We humans will be utterly one with nature only when "things" no longer resist our will, no longer struggle against us.

With age has come a measure of wisdom. Scripture scholars insist that we dare not interpret the Genesis command to "subdue and have dominion" to mean that God has given humankind unrestricted power to do with the earth whatever we will: "The Hebrew term [for 'have dominion'] is used in other places to describe the royal care that characterizes a king as God's vice-regent (Pss 72:8, 110:2; see also Ps 8:5-9). Like ancient kings, men and women are to be the mediators of prosperity and well-being. . . . Reverential care for God's creation rather than exploitation is the mandate given humanity in this section of Genesis." [28] God has given us not despotism but stewardship. And a steward is one who manages what is someone else's. A steward cares, is concerned, agonizes. Stewards may not plunder or waste; they are responsible, can be called to account for their stewardship. "The earth is the Lord's, and all that is in it" (Ps 24:1).

The more deeply I plunge into the Hebrew Testament, the more startled I am by God's covenants that comprise not only humans but an earth alienated from humans by the first sin, corrupted again and again by human rebellion. To begin with, "God saw that the earth was corrupt. . . . And God said to Noah, 'I am determined to make an end of all flesh, for the earth is filled with violence *because of them*' " (Gen 6:12-13). But then I hear God making one covenant with both humans and animals as witness to the bond between all sentient beings: "I am establishing my covenant with you [Noah] and your descendants after you, and *with every living creature that is with you*" (Gen 9:9-10). I hear Hosea expressing God's hope for a return of the original harmony: "I will make for you a covenant on that day with the wild animals, the birds of the air, and the creeping things of the ground" (Hos 2:18).

Then, majestically, Isaiah strides onto center stage, exhorting the exiles in Babylon to a new exodus to their homeland. Here salvation includes the healing of nature, of the environment. As Richard Clifford has put it:

> The new event repeats the old act: a way in the Sea parallels a way in the wilderness; a path in the Mighty Waters parallels paths in the desert. . . . The problem the desert poses to the people is not its lifelessness per se but its interposing itself between Israel and the land; it blocks the people from entering their land. The highway over which the Lord will lead the people will be so safe for humans that the exotic desert animals will join in worship and there will be abundant water for "the people you have formed for yourself." [29]

So intimately is Israel linked to its environment that healing for Israel means healing for nature as well. But only if God's people realize that the twin commands "have dominion" and "subdue the earth" mean not despotic control but reverential care, touching earth and its wonders as God's stewards, "ruling" as God would, in God's place.

Moving into the Common Era, I came to see why, as Clifford has shown, "the basic New Testament proclamation—Jesus Christ has been raised from the dead—is a major statement about human beings' relation to the world." Jesus' rising from the rock is a new creation. It "defeats the primordial enemy of human community in a manner analogous to the first creation in which chaos was defeated and the human race began to live." [30]

In the crucifixion of Christ and his resurrection, the single, triadic community is once again possible: God, humans, and nature (earth, things, the nonrational) in intimate communion. To begin with, men and women. "Whoever is in Christ is a new creation" (2 Cor 5:17). Sin loses not all its power but surely its dominion, its devastating ability to dis-member the human family, so much so that Jesus can pray to his Father, "I in them and you in me, that they may become perfectly one" (Jn 17:23). Through Christ, with Christ, in Christ we can realize God's vision: a human community where no one can say to any other, "I have no need of you" (1 Cor 12:21).

More marvelously still, the community resurrected by Christ does not stop with creatures of intelligence and love. In the Synoptic Gospels, the healing miracles reveal that salvation in Christ means the healing of human beings and their environment. God's "plan for the fullness of time" was "to gather *all things* in [Christ], things in heaven and things on earth" (Eph 1:10). Because nature itself has been corrupted by human sin, St. Paul insists, nature waits for deliverance as anxiously, as eagerly, as we do (Rom 8:18-25).

Precisely what that deliverance means, how it is to be accomplished, what "a new heaven and a new earth" (Rev 21:1) will ultimately look like, this lies beyond our human ken. Still, God's own Word forbids us to rape an earth on which we dance so lightly and so perilously, to pillage creatures of land and sea and sky without which we would perish ingloriously, a product of divine artistry that God saw "was very good" (Gen 1:31). Our imaginative God still has in mind a single community, in which the Creator and all creation live in a harmony that sin cannot substantially corrupt, an interdependence of man, woman, and nature that is an essential facet of salvation's story.

Stewards of earth though we are, we continue to pollute the environment. Fortunately, more and more Americans are beginning to listen to what Jane Blewett has echoed so eloquently: the earth's "call to the human species to learn anew its rightful place among all the other members of the total earth community." [31] Here I simply call attention to an age-old Catholic tradition that sees in nonhuman creation not precisely God's image but still traces *(vestigia)* of the Trinity. In this tradition, only a person with intelligence and the power to love can genuinely image a creating God, but it would be impossible for anything that issues from God's hand not to reflect its Maker in some fashion, not to bear some imprint of the Lord who fashioned it. Because the tradition of *vestigia Dei* is based on theological argumentation far more than on Scripture, I shall defer discussion of image and trace to the next chapter, within the Just Word in Tradition. For the present, it must suffice to insist that, even if only "vestiges" or traces of God's footsteps, the things of earth bear a relationship to God that calls not only for our theological attention but for our Christian reverence.

Salvation within a single, all-embracing community. A shivering, exhilarating awakening: my own salvation depends on fidelity to three relationships: Do I love God above all else? Do I love each sister and brother as Jesus loves me? Do I touch each "thing" (that ice-cold word) with the reverence God asked of humankind at its birthing?

Preaching Biblical Justice

My second question moves us to the preacher: How might we preach more effectively the biblical faith that does justice? Here I offer five suggestions, five realizations.

Appropriation of Scripture

First, to preach the scriptural message persuasively, sheer knowledge, abstract scholarship, is not enough. I must appropriate the biblical texts, make them my own, struggle to make them part of me. The people before me must see, sense, feel that the biblical message is something I live in, breathe, like air. It is not easy, if only because, as my dear deceased Lutheran friend Joseph Sittler insisted,

> Disciplines correlative to preaching can be taught, but preaching as an act of witness cannot be taught. Biblical introduction, training in languages, methods of exegesis, cultural and other historical data that illuminate the texts of the Scriptures—these matters can be refined and transmitted in teaching. But preaching itself, the creative symbiosis within which intersect numberless facts, experiences, insights, felt duties of pastoral obligation toward a specific congregation, the interior existence of the preacher himself, this particular man as he seeks for right utterance of an incommunicable and non-shareable quality of being and thought—this cannot be taught. It is, nevertheless, commanded—and not only by custom of the church.[32]

What, then, is demanded? God's written Word must take hold of me as God's spoken word took hold of Isaiah and Jeremiah, of Ezekiel and Hosea, as the spoken word of Jesus mesmerized Matthew and Mary Magdalene, captured Simon Peter and the Samaritan woman. How? The word I study has to be the word I pray, and the word I pray the word I live.

For most of us, there is no substitute for study of God's Word. I am aware that the founder of the Society of Jesus, Ignatius Loyola, had a single illumination—of God One and Three, the world's fashioning, and the bodying forth of the Son—that outstripped, by his own admission, all he learned or was given by God in sixty-two years. But I cannot count on such a self-manifestation of God. I must have recourse to the source God invented for all of us, the self-disclosure that is God's written Word. It exists not to while away some disenchanted evening but to transform me, to turn me inside out, to fashion a new creature, to put "fire in my belly." If that is so, then the more I know of God's Word and the deeper I plunge into its depths, the more likely I am to experience its incomparable power.

This has uncommon pertinence for effective preaching of justice. I find it ironic that, for the most part, the justice that is preached from the Christian pulpit is ethical justice—allotting to each man, woman, and child what each strictly speaking *deserves*. Ironic that relatively few preachers are aware that the justice demanded of believers assumes the ethical but transcends it. Few realize that we are called to preach not simply or primarily distributive or commutative justice, or only God's Decalogue (don't kill or steal, don't covet another's property or wife), but fidelity to all the relationships and responsibilities that stem from our covenant with God in Christ. Few have discovered by serious study that biblical fidelity comprises our responsibilities to all that is: to God, to our sisters and brothers, to nonhuman creation.

And yet, even study, an organized, disciplined approach to Scripture, is not enough. Martin Luther was right on target when he called for contemplation of each word of God in silence. "Go to the Bible itself, dear Christians, and let my expositions and those of all scholars be no more than a tool with which to build aright, so that we can understand, taste, and abide in the simple and pure word of God."[33] For the Bible differs from Blackstone's *Commentaries* and Einstein's theory of relativity; it is a book to be prayed.

What I am commending to each preacher is a spirituality that is biblically based. I mean a reverent immersion in Scripture such that intelligence is subservient to love. We Christians do fairly well with the Gospels. But to limit myself to the Gospels, or the Gospels and John Chrysostom's beloved St. Paul, is like skipping to the last chapter of an Agatha Christie mystery. We should be nourished by all that has gone before: by a God who walked with Adam and Eve in the cool of evening, walked with a select people through the Red Sea; by a God who was Father and Savior and Lover long before the Son of God took our flesh; by singers of psalms and prophets of doom and deliverance; by Israel's journeying to God through faith and infidelity, through wisdom and purification.[34]

No doubt, a consummate artist could conceivably con a congregation with a sermon crafted completely from scriptural scholarship. But the faithful at worship are as little impressed by sheer learning as they are by irrational ranting. They must sense from the way I speak that God's continual call for justice, the Psalmist's "Happy are those who observe justice" (Ps 106:3), the Isaian "Let the oppressed go free" (Isa 58:6), Jesus' preference for compassion over sacrifice, these have gotten into my gut; I am obviously trying to live Jesus' declared mission, not only struggling to "*preach* good news to the poor, *proclaim* release for prisoners and sight for the blind," but actually trying to "send the downtrodden away relieved" (Lk 4:18).

Conversion

A second suggestion, a second realization, intimately tied to the first: powerful biblical preaching calls for conversion within the preacher. Not necessarily a sudden lightning bolt; more commonly a ceaseless turning to Christ. I do not claim that it is impossible to preach effectively about justice from an ethical motive, a philosophical conviction that to be genuinely human is to care deeply, to recognize in other women and men one's sisters and brothers. Some ethical humanists have lived such a realization admirably. But within a Christian vision, preaching justice involves a disciple's effort to follow the Christ who came to call sinners, the Christ who had a special empathy for the underprivileged, the Christ who for his final three years was homeless, the Christ who lived and died for the soldiers who gambled for his garments as much as for the mother who had wrapped him in swaddling clothes. Within a Christian vision, I preach justice most effectively when I love as Jesus loved.

Second Great Commandment

A third suggestion, a third realization: given the inclination of Christians to see justice as a secular activity, an ethical construct that flows not from divine revelation but from human philosophy, from ethics, it is imperative that we who preach persuade those who listen that biblical justice is in large part an effort to implement the second great commandment of the law and the gospel, "You shall love your neighbor as yourself" (Lev 19:18; Mt 22:39)—the commandment which Jesus said is "like" the first, is "like" loving God. Here I make bold to recommend the highly Christian vision of evangelization that Pope Paul VI outlined back in 1975. In a remarkable apostolic exhortation, *Evangelization in the Modern World,* he impressed on the Catholic faithful two realities utterly inseparable from evangelization: Jesus Christ and people.

As Paul VI insisted, "Evangelization will always have as the foundation, center, and supreme focus of its dynamism the clear proclamation that in Jesus Christ . . . salvation is offered to every human being as a gracious gift inspired by God's mercy." But, once having anchored evangelization in the centrality of Christ, the pontiff went on to declare:

> Evangelization cannot be complete . . . unless account is taken of the links between the gospel and the concrete personal and social life of men and women. . . . In proclaiming liberation and ranging herself with all who suffer and toil for it, the Church cannot allow herself or her mission to be limited to the purely religious sphere while she ignores the temporal problems of the human person. . . . The Church considers it highly important to establish structures which are more human, more just, more respectful of the rights of the person, less oppressive and coercive.[35]

But we always return to the overriding issue: What precisely is the justice we are preaching? Not simply, not primarily, a justice that emerges from philosophy or from law: Give to others what they can prove they deserve. Preach this alone, and our people may well be justified when they ask, Where is the gospel of God in all this? They have not trudged into God's house for a class in ethics, for a debate on the rights of women on welfare, for a plea on behalf of United Way, a specific strategy for housing the homeless. What they are seeking from me, justifiably, is a soul-piercing word that conveys what a revealing God expects of them, a justice that mimics God's own fidelity to God's promises, God's special care for the helpless and hopeless, the God who, the Psalmist insists, "hears the cry of the poor."

The Poor and the Predicament of the Prosperous

A fourth suggestion, a fourth realization: it is not only the economically disadvantaged that fall under the rubric *poor.* Cast a swift glance back into the Bible. Poor is the leper, ostracized from society, excluded from normal association with others, compelled often to live outside his town. Poor is the widow, who could not inherit from her husband, was an obvious victim for the exactions of a creditor, had no defender at law and so was often at the mercy of dishonest judges. Poor are the orphans with no parents to love them. Poor is the sinful woman who bathed Jesus' feet with her tears, the woman caught in the very act of adultery, to be stoned according to the law of Moses. Israel's poor were the afflicted, those of a lower class oppressed by the powerful.[36] The poor were all those on whose behalf the Lord castigated the chosen people through the prophets:

Cease to do evil,
    learn to do good;
seek justice,
    rescue the oppressed,
defend the orphan,
    plead for the widow. (Isa 1:16-17)

Besides the obviously poor, I suggest that the word can be extended to embrace what has been called "the predicament of the prosperous." In a genuine sense, poor was wealthy toll collector Zacchaeus, a henchman of the Romans, a social outcast because of his job, no longer a true "son of Abraham." In our time, the poor include a megabucks entertainer Michael Jackson, a Haiti President Jean Aristide, a Senator Bob Packwood, a CBS president Laurence Tisch, a presidential wife Hillary Clinton, a D.C. Mayor Barry, a Cardinal Joseph Bernardin, a Supreme Court Justice Sandra Day O'Connor, and so on and so forth. They carry on the biblical examples, the peculiar difficulties that confront the rich and the powerful as they struggle to enter the kingdom. Not the prerogative of the preacher, therefore, to sympathize with the economically poor and the powerless while castigating the wealthy and "the high and mighty," "the bold and the beautiful." All need our loving concern. All demand of the preacher the skillful approach Jesus took to differing needs: to Zacchaeus with his wealth as well as the widow with her mite; to the centurion with his sick boy as well as the robber crucified at his right hand; to Pilate washing his hands of him as well as the woman taken in adultery.

Justice as Lens for Seeing All of Reality

This introduces a fifth suggestion, a final realization: often the most effective way of preaching biblical justice is not to utter the word *justice* at all. Why? Because, for all too many, justice is limited to punishment deservedly handed out to criminals. Because untold numbers of Christians are turned off by the word, despite its constant recurrence in Scripture. Even more importantly, because justice should be less a separate category than a lens through which we see all of reality. And a lens it should be; for biblical justice comprises fidelity to all our covenant relationships: to God, to humans, to the earth.

In consequence, I tend to preach about biblical justice in the concrete, in terms that speak to our people's everyday concerns. Take one example. In 1991, on the feast of the Epiphany, after treating the Isaian (60:1-6) and Matthean (2:1-12) readings, I developed my third and final point in part as follows:[37]

Yes, Epiphany celebrates God manifesting, revealing Godself to the world in Christ. But how did God manifest Godself, reveal Godself in Christ? As a child. Whom did the astrologers from the East adore on their knees? A child. The Son of God was born as we are, came from a mother's body, became what each of us grownups once was. That is basically why Christmas is so special for children, why we delight in toys for children, in Santa Claus with a child on each knee, in baby Jesus clothed like a king, in the Vienna Boys Choir, in pyjama-clad children opening gifts around a tree, children on sleighs, children enveloped in love.

But the Christ child raises a problem. Pope John Paul II put it bluntly: "In the Christian view, our treatment of children becomes a measure of our fidelity to the Lord himself,"[38] the Lord who asserted, "Whoever receives one such child in my name receives me" (Mt 18:5). In the next 60 seconds, 27 children under five will die in developing countries—almost 40,000 each day. And they will die mostly from diseases we know how to prevent—measles, diarrhea, respiratory infections. In this decade, the '90s, do you know how many children will die needlessly? 150 million.

[But] we need not fly to Ethiopia, to Cambodia, to the sub-Sahara to find "no room in the inn" for children. If you take the latest available data in six categories—infant mortality, child abuse, children in poverty, teenage suicide, teenage drug abuse, and high-school dropouts—in our own land of power and prosperity their social well-being reached a new low in 1987, "the worst year for children in two decades."[39]

We treat them like statistics, these children for whom the Child was born, for whom he bled. . . . We forget what the Second Vatican Council saw so clearly: "The future of humanity lies in the hands of those who are strong enough to provide coming generations with reasons for living and hoping"—our hands.[40]

Have I forgotten Isaiah, forgotten the adoring Magi? Not at all. The prophet continues to protest that "justice is far from us" (Isa 59:9). He might even suggest that we "walk in gloom" as long as "25 percent of America's children under six live in poverty," as long as hundreds are born with AIDS or addicted to cocaine or crack, as long as on our own streets "a child is injured or killed by a gun every 36 minutes."[41] There is no point in offering the Christ child "gold and frankincense and myrrh" (Mt 2:11) if D.C.'s children for whom he was born are hollow-eyed from hunger, if black children have to beg for the crumbs that fall from white tables.

I concluded: "Only if we love our sisters and brothers at least as much as we love ourselves can our native gloom be transfigured into graced glory. Only then can we really say that in Christ, God has indeed manifested Godself to the world, to us. Reach out to just one of these little ones, and you can sing with sincerity, 'Unto us a child is born.' The Christ child."

This is what I mean by preaching biblical justice without naming it. It is God's care for the scriptural orphan transposed to America of the 1990s. It is a responsibility imposed on us by the covenant that was cut in Christ's blood. The child born with a drug addiction, the child growing up hungry, the child sexually abused, the child gunned down by teenage gangsters— here is Christ crucified again; here is the Christ to whom the Christian must play Christ. No one of us dare mouth with Cain, "Am I my brother's keeper?" (Gen 4:9). For if we pass by on the other side, the Lord will thunder to us, as he thundered to Cain, "What have you done? Listen; your brother's blood, your sister's blood, is crying out to me from the ground" (v. 10).

A swift summary. When we preach justice in a Christian context, ethical justice and legal justice simply scratch the surface of social justice. It does not take a committed Christian to give to a man, woman, or child what he or she can claim as a strict right, what is laid down in law or can be deduced by the light of reason. What we preach is not Aristotle or Blackstone; we preach Christ. And in preaching Christ, we preach what Christ was cruci-fied for. And what was that? Among much else, to let us see in his flesh, to see in Bethlehem and on Calvary, how precious each human person is in God's sight, to realize that Paul was speaking not simply of himself but of every human ever fashioned of God's love when he cried, "The Son of God loved me and gave himself for me" (Gal 2:20).

Realization, however, is only a splendid beginning. What I know with my head and feel in my bones must pressure me to passionate preaching. Of all the demands on preachers, none is more urgent today than a persua-sive presentation of biblical justice. On the whole, the Christian faithful are aware that without the *first* commandment of the law and the gospel salvation is impossible. Unless they love God, their religion is mockery. For there lies a Christian's primary and ultimate fidelity. What has not pene-trated with equal force, what we who preach have been less successful in advertising, is the commandment that Jesus said "is like" the first: the de-mand that we love our sisters and brothers as if we were standing in the very shoes of the less fortunate. It is basically the still more startling com-mandment that we love them as Jesus has loved us—even unto crucifixion. And in a sense there is a third commandment that carries us back to the first chapter of God's Book: take reverent care, a steward's care, of the earth, of all creation, of every creature that God has so lovingly shaped; for "the earth is the Lord's."

Without the biblical justice that is fidelity to the relationships imposed by our covenant with God in Christ, any and every claim to love God is itself a mockery. Each Christian community, each parish, must gather to ask three pungent questions: (1) What are the problem areas, the injustice issues, within our territory? (2) What resources lie at our fingertips to con-front these issues? (3) What, concretely, shall we do?

But I dare not lay this burden on my people if I myself have not been profoundly changed, if I have not begun to follow the Christ whose dying for his crucified images began when he came forth from Mary in Bethle-hem. Very simply, the faithful who listen to me must somehow sense that, like Isaiah and Jesus, I agonize over, am tormented by, every single injus-tice that keeps a brother or sister from living as God's beloved image on earth, that ravages and rapes what our Lord of love has so imaginatively

TWO

Preaching the Just Word
in Tradition

When Notre Dame's Lawrence Cunningham was professor of religion
at Florida State, he found himself frustrated in the classroom. Why?

> . . . because students lack any sense of the historical perspective of West-
> ern culture in general and the part Catholicism played in the formation
> of that culture in particular. They . . . have no sense of the kind of
> church which existed before the Second Vatican Council. Students have
> this strong conviction that what is important happens now and the "now"
> has little or no link with the past. They tend to see the life of the church
> rather as they see the surface of a video game screen: active, immediate
> and graspable as a whole.[1]

Professor Cunningham's jeremiad is a pertinent preface to a presentation that moves us from biblical justice to its development in the succeed-
ing centuries, during the Common Era. Pertinent because it focuses our
attention on a precious but poorly understood and much maligned reality:
tradition.[2] Once again I have found it useful to divide my presentation into
two segments, two questions: (1) What has tradition to do with justice—

with social justice, specifically the social justice that is biblical? (2) How, by all that is good and holy, does anyone preach a tradition?

Justice in Tradition

My first question: what has tradition to do with justice? Before all else, let me explain what I mean by tradition. Not tradition as some musty museum piece, "This is the way we've always done it." Not tradition as including everything that has encumbered, embarrassed Christian history, from the repressive state church through the Inquisition to our four and a half centuries of internecine Christian hostility. I mean tradition as the best of our past, infused with the insights of the present, with a view to a richer, more catholic future.

A sad, perhaps fatal facet of contemporary Catholicism is massive ignorance. More highly educated than ever, most of our educated Catholics, including clerics, lack a sense of Catholic tradition. The results are already tangible: a generation of Catholic college and university graduates who know Augustine only as a born-again Catholic who foisted on us a hellish doctrine of original sin and a pessimistic view of sex and marriage; who cannot spell Chalcedon, even though three decades ago Harvey Cox argued that apart from the Council of Chalcedon technopolis is unintelligible; who can anathematize Aquinas and scuttle Scholasticism without ever having read a word thereof; who sneer at the mere mention of "medieval," as if the Middle Ages were darker than our own; who could not care less about a papal pronouncement, much less peruse it. During more than a half-century of theology I have watched our incredibly rich tradition pass slowly but surely into museums or, at best, into the hands of appreciative Protestant sisters and brothers.

The result for social justice? I am embarrassingly aware of a recent aphorism: Catholic teaching on social justice is "our best-kept secret." I shall speak first of our early tradition, an experience that Rome and Geneva treasure in common; then a "social gospel" more familiar to Protestants than to Catholics; finally a word about a more recent Catholic tradition that unfortunately is not shared explicitly in our current disunity.

Patristic Tradition

Countless "educated" Catholics are utterly unaware that the miraculous triumph of early Christianity was due in large measure to a radical sense of community.[3] Indispensable facets of this communitarian sense were a conviction and a practice: a conviction about the proper use of material possessions, and impressive practical aid to the needy. Here five themes are of paramount importance:[4]

First, Christianity had to transform the values of the Greco-Roman world it inhabited. Specifically, an attitude toward property, possessions. Listen to one early document: "Do not turn away from the needy; rather, share everything with your brother, and do not say, 'It is private property.' If you are sharers in what is imperishable, how much more so in the things that perish!"[5] The value? Sharing rather than possessing.

Second, to attain that attitude, a conversion of the human heart is indispensable. To become genuine Christians, the rich must become detached from their riches. Particularly impressive in this regard is Clement of Alexandria, who succeeded Pantaenus as head of the catechetical school in that cosmopolitan city about the year 200. His homily *The Rich Man's Salvation* is a courageous, realistic, if not always exegetically defensible effort to confront difficulties faced by the prosperous among the faithful in a literal interpretation of such Gospel commands as "If you wish to be perfect, go, sell your possessions, and give the money to the poor" (Mt 19:21). He insists that the text cannot intend to exclude the wealthy from God's kingdom. What, then, does it mean?

> It is not, as some hastily take it to be, a command that [the rich young man] should throw away the property that belongs to him and renounce his wealth. What he is told to banish from his soul are his beliefs about wealth, his attachment to it, his excessive desire for it, his diseased excitement over it and his anxious cares—those thorns of earthly existence which choke the seed of true life. There is nothing marvellous or enviable about having no money, unless true life be the reason for it. . . .
>
> It is possible for a man to unburden himself of his wealth and to remain none the less sunk in habitual desire and hankering for it. . . . How much better are the possibilities of the opposite condition, in which one not only possesses enough not to have to worry about possessions oneself, but can also aid others as one ought. How much opportunity would men still have for sharing their goods, if no one had any? . . .

Wealth is an instrument. . . . You can use it justly; then it will serve justice. If it is used unjustly, it will be the servant of injustice. . . . So what is to be destroyed is not one's possessions but the passions of the soul, which hinder the right use of one's belongings. . . .

Imagine a man who holds his possessions, his gold, silver and houses, as gifts from God; who serves the God who gave them by using them for the welfare of mankind; who knows that he possesses them for his brothers' sakes rather than his own; who is superior to and not the slave of his possessions; who does not go around with his possessions in his heart or let them determine the horizons of his life; who is always engaged on some fine and holy work; and who, if he comes to be deprived of them, can bear their loss as cheerfully as their abundance. Such a man is the one whom the Lord calls blessed and poor in spirit. He is the one who is fit to be an inheritor of the kingdom of heaven.[6]

There is only one reason, declares a second-century author, why God allows some Christians to be wealthy: "to perform [a] ministry [to the poor] for Him."[7] What can motivate men and women to such detachment, to be at once affluent and poor in spirit? If they are in love with God, with Christ, with their sisters and brothers. Here a remarkably original thinker, Origen, waxed passionate in his effort to liberate the rich from the acquisitiveness, the greed, that the early Church regarded as a form of idolatry:

God . . . knows that what a man loves with all his heart and soul and might—this for him is God. Let each one of us now examine himself and silently in his own heart decide which is the flame of love that chiefly and above all else is afire within him, which is the passion that he finds he cherishes more keenly than all others. . . . Whatever it is that weighs the heaviest in the balance of your affection, that for you is God. But I fear that with very many the love of gold will turn the scale, that down will come the weight of covetousness lying heavy in the balance.[8]

Third, basic to the fresh Christian attitude is a traditional patristic belief: God created the material universe for all humankind; the rich are essentially earth's stewards. Listen to a remarkably pastoral fourth-century bishop, Ambrose of Milan: "God has ordered all things to be produced so that there should be food in common for all, and that the earth should be the common possession of all. Nature, therefore, has produced a common right for all, but greed has made it a right for the few."[9] To Ambrose, the Old Testament tale of Ahab and Naboth (1 Kgs 21:1–29) is a human constant: "Ahab is not one person, someone born long ago; every day, alas, the world sees Ahabs reborn, never to die out. . . . Neither is Naboth one person, a poor man once murdered; every day some Naboth is done to death, every day the poor are murdered." [10]

Important here is a significant realization: the Fathers denied not the right to private property but its greedy misuse. In John Chrysostom's words, the rich they attacked "are not the rich as such, only those who misuse their wealth." [11] Still, many of the fourth-century Church Fathers saw in private property a root of human dissension; in the struggle for possessions they found a subversion of God's original order. John Chrysostom is a powerful example. In a "wise dispensation" God

has made certain things common, as the sun, air, earth, and water . . . whose benefits are dispensed equally to all as brethren. . . . Observe that concerning things that are common there is no contention, but all is peaceable. But when one attempts to possess himself of anything, to make it his own, then contention is introduced, as if nature herself were indignant, that when God brings us together in every way, we are eager to divide and separate ourselves by appropriating things, and by using those cold words "mine and thine." Then there is contention and uneasiness. But where this is not, no strife or contention is bred. This state therefore is rather our inheritance, and more agreeable to nature.[12]

Fourth, an especially powerful motive: the presence of Christ in—Christ identified with—the impoverished and disadvantaged. Here Chrysostom and Augustine wed practical theology and impassioned rhetoric. Chrysostom declares that the poor are more venerable an altar than the altar of stone on which the Sacrifice is offered, on which the body of Christ rests.

This altar [the poor] is composed of the very members of Christ, and the Lord's Body becomes an altar for you. . . . This altar is more awesome than the altar in this church. . . . The altar [of stone] becomes holy because it receives the body of Christ; the altar [of the poor] because it is the Body of Christ. Therefore it is more awesome than the altar near which you, a layperson, are standing. . . . This altar you can see set up everywhere, in the lane and in the market, and at any hour you may sacrifice thereon; for here too sacrifice is consummated.[13]

Little wonder that Chrysostom urged his people to cover the naked Christ before they ornamented his table, forbade them to make a golden cup for

Christ while they were refusing him a cup of cold water. "Don't neglect your brother in his distress while you decorate his house. Your brother is more truly his temple than any church building."[14]

Similarly for Augustine, more profoundly theological than Chrysostom, but like him the pastor and preacher. For Augustine, "love cannot be divided." Love the children of God, and you love the Son of God; love the Son of God, and you love the Father. Conversely, you dare not say, you cannot say, that you love Christ if you love not the members of Christ—all his members, without discrimination.[15] And lest we think he is limiting our love to orthodox believers, Augustine insists that the love of Catholics must be utterly catholic—offered, that is, as the grace of God is offered, to all:

> Love all men, even your enemies; love them, not because they are your brothers, but that they may become your brothers—so that you may ever burn with brotherly love, whether for him who is already your brother, or for your enemy, that he may by [your] loving become your brother. . . . Even he who does not yet believe in Christ . . . love him, and love him with brotherly love. He is not yet your brother, but you love him precisely that he may be your brother. All our love, therefore, is brotherly love toward Christians, toward all Christ's members.[16]

Some, Augustine sorrows, "would limit love to the land of Africa!" No, he protests. "Extend your love over the entire earth, if you would love Christ; for the members of Christ lie all over the earth."[17]

Fifth, the Church of Christ is a community of support and sharing. It is not only the poor, the disadvantaged, the marginalized that benefit from the generosity of the materially fortunate. The orphan and the aged and the widow, wearing what Clement of Alexandria called "the uniform of love," become "the spiritual bodyguard" of the rich—a return of love that could take many forms: nursing care, intercessory prayer, a kindly word of counsel, even a stinging word of protest.[18]

This is what the early Church not only believed but preached—preached within the liturgy and beyond. And preached because the Fathers of the Church saw themselves primarily not as philosophers or sociologists but as "enlightened interpreters of the Bible, which contains God's saving revelation."[19]

Protestant Social Gospel

Of the Social Gospel, the movement that began within American Protestantism in the second half of the nineteenth century, I must speak somewhat hesitantly—high in my admiration, woeful in my ignorance.[20] The Social Gospel was basically a social movement that only gradually developed a theology. It was "American Protestantism's response to the challenge of modern industrial society," a society "characterized by the rise of large-scale production units that drew together vast proletarian populations in hastily built, overcrowded cities."[21] The social context out of which the theology emerged makes for distressing reading:

Technological unemployment, immigration, and other factors combined by 1900 to create a standing army of a million unemployed whereas in 1870 the labor supply had been inadequate. The demands of industry brought millions from the farms and from the old world to the new and crowded cities, expanding the working classes fivefold. Between 1860 and 1890 the national wealth increased from sixteen to seventy-eight and one half billions of dollars, more than half of which was held by some forty thousand families or one third of one percent of the population. But in the decade 1870–80 real wages, which had never been above the bare subsistence level, had declined from an average of $400 to $300, forcing children to premature labor and driving women to the factories beside the men. The American industrial revolution, in the process of creating wealth such as the world had never seen or dreamed of, produced also a sullen proletariat resentful of the poverty it had obtained as its share of the bounty, and the republic of Jefferson and Jackson now became the scene of the most embittered class wars and the most glaring social contrasts modern times had seen.[22]

At the same time, labor leaders and others were assailing Christianity as a class religion concerned to protect private property and indifferent to human ills. A fresh interpretation of Jesus' message was surely in order, perhaps inevitable—a Christianity that addressed itself to slums and sweatshops, to company towns and unemployment.

Significant here is what the movement had for objectives: (1) to respond to the challenges presented by the abuses of industrialism, (2) to serve as a corrective to the theological individualism and economic conservatism of the churches, and (3) to insist that a just social order can be fashioned from the teachings of Jesus. But it was not the academy that initiated the Social

Gospel; it was "the practical experience of Protestant ministers working in urban situations and realizing that the individualistic piety and preaching for which they had been trained was of little help in dealing with the urban poor." [23] It was not simply individual sinfulness but the system that was responsible for the social misery. That is why the ministers turned their attention first to the social structures. Only later did they sense with Walter Rauschenbusch, the most remarkable exponent of the movement's theology, that "we have a social Gospel. We need a systematic theology large enough to match it and vital enough to back it." [24]

What Rauschenbusch, together with Horace Bushnell, Shailer Mathews, and others, saw as imperative was a new social order that reflected the fatherhood of God and the brotherhood of man. Their efforts climaxed in December 1908, when the overwhelming majority of churches of the evangelical tradition formed the National (then Federal) Council of Churches in the USA. Why? As the preamble to its constitution declared, to secure "a larger combined influence for the Churches of Christ in all matters affecting the moral and social condition of the people, so as to promote the application of the law of Christ in every relation of human life."

To the credit of the Social Gospel, many of the reforms it advocated have been written into national legislation. True, the movement as such did not endure. For this several reasons have been adduced: (1) Its exponents oversimplified the essential goodness of the human person and his/her responsiveness to moral persuasion. (2) They failed to realize "the magnitude and complexity of the problems they optimistically 'solved,'" and this led to a broad lack of confidence in their solutions.[25] (3) Much of their energy was dissipated in efforts to impose national Prohibition. (4) The movement was further weakened when disciples of Karl Barth attacked the theological adequacy of the Social Gospel, and Reinhold Niebuhr assailed its political naïveté.

John Bennett has pointed out that the movement as a whole was too optimistic in its view of history, did not have a sense of "the depth and stubbornness of sin and evil," too facilely identified the kingdom of God with a particular social objective, did not consistently preserve the transcendence of the kingdom as beyond history and as a judgment on history, and was little concerned with racism and women's liberation.[26]

Nevertheless, in its concern for justice and its activist emphasis, the

Social Gospel "left a characteristic stamp on American Protestantism."[27] And it is not insignificant to find Martin Luther King Jr. reporting that Rauschenbusch had influenced his thinking.[28] In fact, it has been argued that the Social Gospel should be redefined in terms of the continuing quest for social justice that has persisted through and after neo-orthodoxy, has manifested itself again in the civil rights movement, and is a continuing thread in American Christianity.[29]

In 1980 the theologian T. Howland Sanks of the Jesuit School of Theology at Berkeley discovered enough prima facie similarities between the Social Gospel and Latin American liberation theology to warrant a study of Rauschenbusch and Gustavo Gutiérrez, one of the earliest of the liberation theologians and arguably quite representative of the movement at its best.[30] Sanks uncovered similarities and differences.

Similarities indeed: (1) Both the Social Gospel and liberation theology reject a spiritualized understanding of the gospel, repudiate excessive individualism, are convinced that salvation is social, that God's kingdom can be achieved only by striving for righteousness in the world. (2) Both display a sense of urgency, see social justice as today's voice of prophecy, are convinced that their theologies are the wave of the future, are anticapitalist, seem open to some form of socialism, possibly even of a Marxist type.[31]

Still, Sanks sees significant differences: (1) The oppression that concerns liberation theologians is not only economic but political. It stems not only from capital-labor conflict but from economic exploitation of the Third World by the First, from neocolonialism, from class consciousness and divisions. (2) The Roman Catholic Church has more institutional influence in Latin America than did the Protestant churches in the United States. With a less pluralistic culture, organized religion in Latin America has greater potential for influencing political and economic conditions. (3) Liberation theologians, unlike the Social Gospelers, foresee the need for some form of revolution (not necessarily violent) rather than a gradual evolution through the economic and political systems already in place. (4) Liberation theologians are less optimistic than were the Social Gospel theologians about Christianizing the social order, more sophisticated in their understanding and critique of ideologies, less likely to identify the Christian ideal with some particular social movement or program. (5) Liberation theology is more concerned with a theological vision than with social ethics.[32]

Modern Catholic Teaching

This brief venture into Latin American liberation theology may serve as a transition to a rich, extensive Catholic tradition that unfortunately is not shared explicitly in our current Christian disunity—perhaps even more regrettably, is a remarkably well-kept secret within Roman Catholicism. Here I shall stress official documents, well aware that official documents, for all their significance, are hardly the whole story, do not reveal the length and breadth of Catholic theory and activism in the area of social justice. But they do constitute the bulk of the building blocks of modern Catholic social teaching.[33]

Indeed a well-kept secret. Save for professionals, our postimmigrant Catholicism has rarely heard Pope Leo XIII, in the context of greed and exploitation, affirm private property and the common purpose of property, distinguish just ownership from just use, declare the obligation of employers to pay a living wage, proclaim workers' rights to organize for group protection, insist on collaboration rather than class struggle as the fundamental means for social change. His encyclical *Rerum novarum (On the Condition of Labor)* was a burning cry of protest against the exploitation of poor workers, a solemn rejection in 1891 of a dominant economic tenet of the times, "that labour is a commodity to be bought at market prices determined by the law of supply and demand rather than by the human needs of the worker."[34] One example of Leo's courageous, forceful initiative:

A characteristic of a well-constituted state is an abundance of material goods.... Such goods cannot be provided without the highly productive, skilled, and painstaking labor of the unpropertied workers who are employed in farms and factories. So great is their vigor and efficiency in this regard that it may truly be said that it is only by the labor of workingmen that states grow rich. Equity requires of the state, therefore, that it have particular regard for the unpropertied workers, so that those who bring so much of advantage to the community should themselves be well housed and clothed, enjoy greater comfort, and suffer less hardship. Whence it follows that measures are to be supported which are seen in some way to offer an improvement of the condition of the workers. Such solicitude is far from being harmful to others. Rather, it is greatly beneficial to the whole community, for it is of great importance to the state that those from whom such necessary goods proceed are not themselves made wretched in every way.[35]

This is not to say that *Rerum novarum* is beyond criticism. Michael Walsh of Heythrop College, University of London, has said it is difficult today to understand the impact of what seems so old-fashioned a document—its nostalgia for a medieval past, the Thomism that is its philosophical context, and Catholics with their own unions. Still, in point of fact, "it decisively shaped social teaching down almost to the present day. Only Pope John Paul II has stepped outside it."[36]

Our postimmigrant Catholicism has rarely heard Pope Pius XI, in the context of the Great Depression, raise concerns about the viability of the Western economic system after a period of apparent success. Forty years after *Rerum novarum*, his 1931 encyclical *Quadragesimo anno (On Reconstructing the Social Order)* upheld private property against collectivism but stressed social responsibility; it proposed just wages as a family wage, even a workers' share in ownership and profits. Strikingly, Pius introduced a critical concept in the development of Catholic social teaching, subsidiarity:

> As history abundantly proves, it is true that on account of changed conditions many things which were done by small associations in former times cannot be done now save by large associations. Still, that most weighty principle, which cannot be set aside or changed, remains fixed and unshaken in social philosophy. Just as it is gravely wrong to take from individuals what they can accomplish by their own initiative and industry and give it to the community, so also it is an injustice and at the same time a grave evil and disturbance of right order to assign to a greater and higher association what lesser and subordinate organizations can do. For every social activity ought of its very nature to furnish help to the members of the body social, and never destroy or absorb them.[37]

Our postimmigrant Catholicism has rarely heard Pope Pius XII concede that private property is a natural right, yet argue that private property remains subordinated to a more fundamental right, the basic right every human being has to whatever material needs are necessary for full development as a person.[38] Our postimmigrant Catholicism has rarely heard Pope John XXIII describe in 1961 a feature of industrialized society wherein people's lives were increasingly shaped by institutions: unions, governments, laws, school systems, companies. His *Mater et magistra (Christianity and Social Progress)*, in perhaps its most significant innovation, allotted the state a much larger role in the lives of its citizens, especially in matters of welfare. He put state action on a par with private initiative in achieving the social responsibility of property:

> The present advance in scientific knowledge and productive technology clearly puts it within the power of the public authority to a much greater degree than ever before to reduce imbalances which may exist between different branches of the economy or between different regions within the same company or even between the different peoples of the world. It also puts into the hands of public authority a greater means for limiting fluctuations in the economy and for providing effective measures to prevent the recurrence of mass unemployment. Hence the insistent demands on those in authority—since they are responsible for the common good—to increase the degree and scope of their activities in the economic sphere, and to devise ways and means and set the necessary machinery in motion for the attainment of this end.
>
> But however extensive and far-reaching the influence of the state on the economy may be, it must never be exerted to the extent of depriving the individual citizen of his freedom of action.[39]

Freedom of action. It reminds me that John XXIII made another significant contribution to a reconstruction of the social order. Through many decades, in its efforts to construct a livable, viable social order, the Catholic Church did well to stress three facets of human living: truth, justice, and love. For all their importance, however, these have proved insufficient. All over the world, in our own dear country as well, all too many men, women, and children still go to bed hungry; all too many continue to lust for the blood of other humans; all too many are refused a human existence because the color of their skin makes them second-class citizens. Many reasons conspire to explain so unjust a world order. But as far back as 1972 I was persuaded that one formidable factor has rarely been highlighted enough. It was only with John XXIII that the Catholic Church put on the same level with truth, justice, and love a fourth principle of social order to structure our philosophy of society and state: freedom.[40]

Now freedom has a rich history within Catholic thought. It has long been part of my philosophical and theological baggage: the free disobedience of the first man that originated our sinful schizophrenia; the free obedience of Christ that makes the children of God genuinely free; the psychological freedom, the inner yes or no, that makes me human; the free commitment to Christ that makes me Christian. All this and so much more.

The problem is, our accent has been on the inner core of freedom; little accent on the external conditions that make it possible for a man or woman to be free, to live freely, to act in freedom. Why, it took the Catholic Church till 1965 to catch up with the nineteenth century, to declare officially that religious freedom is a human right, that "the very dignity of the human person" demands that "in matters religious no one is to be forced to act in a manner contrary to his/her own beliefs, nor is anyone to be restrained from acting in accordance with his/her own beliefs, whether privately or publicly, whether alone or in association with others, within due limits." [41] Over the centuries the Catholic Church was dreadfully reluctant to state publicly that man and woman must be allowed to seize more and more the reins of their destiny, directing it toward a society where they will be free of *every* kind of slavery. Reluctant to recognize that in the building of a social order truth, justice, and love are not enough if the man and woman they serve are not free; in fact, that truth, justice, and love are not really there if the persons they serve are not actually, genuinely free. Until John XXIII . . .

Very much in line with his stress on freedom in action, and only a few months before his death on June 3, 1963, John XXIII's *Pacem in terris (Peace on Earth)* introduced the concept of economic rights, drawn from an analysis of human dignity. His "right to life" included adequate food, clothing, shelter, rest, medical care, social services, some form of "security." He noted with deep sorrow an arms race that threatened economic justice, an economic injustice that threatened peace. He called for a reduction of arms stockpiles across the world, a ban on nuclear weaponry.

Our postimmigrant Catholicism has rarely read perhaps the most important document of Vatican II, the most authoritative in Catholic social teaching, *Gaudium et spes (The Church in the Modern World,* 1965). It is the first time the magisterium (here the collective body of bishops with and under the pope) has spoken so fully about the temporal aspects of Christian living: marriage and family life, overpopulation, responsible parenthood, respect for life, cultural diversity and development. Under socioeconomic life the council discussed fundamental imbalances between rich and poor, requirements of justice, share of earthly goods for all, the common good. It legitimated nonviolence and conscientious objection; it rejected blind obedience to commands, wars of subjugation, acts of war directed at centers of population. It condemned the arms race as a trap for humanity and devastation for the poor. It put the Church squarely at the service of humanity: "Christians cannot yearn for anything more ardently than to serve the people of the modern world ever more generously and effectively." [42]

Our postimmigrant Catholicism has rarely heard Pope Paul VI on *The Development of Peoples* (*Populorum progressio,* 1967). With the social question shifting from a focus on rich and poor individuals to rich and poor nations, with Russia and the United States vying for influence in newly independent nations, Paul urged immediate action to build a just economic order, not on the principles of liberalistic capitalism, but on solidarity between rich and poor, dialogue, universal love, a retention of the competitive market, and structural changes. Eight years later, in a remarkable apostolic exhortation titled *Evangelii nuntiandi* (*Evangelization in the Modern World,* 1975), Paul insisted that two realities are inseparable from evangelization: Jesus Christ and people. Jesus Christ, because without Christ as the centerpiece, there is no genuine evangelization. People, because "evangelization cannot be complete unless account is taken of the links between the gospel and the concrete personal and social life of men and women. . . . The Church considers it highly important to establish structures which are more human, more just, more respectful of the rights of the person, less oppressive and coercive." [43]

Especially significant is Paul VI's 1971 letter to Maurice Cardinal Roy, president of the Pontifical Commission Justitia et Pax, marking the eightieth anniversary of *Rerum novarum.* Entitled *Octogesima adveniens (A Call to Action),* it named new social problems: urbanization, the role of youth, women's equality, the marginalized new poor, discrimination, immigration, unemployment, the media, environmental exploitation. But the letter is uncommonly significant because it reveals Paul's awareness of the importance of human experience, of the historical context, for any ecclesial reflection or action. Largely from his own extensive travels (the United States, India, Turkey, Portugal, Colombia, Uganda), firsthand experiences of the diverse situations in which Christians found themselves, Paul could write this striking paragraph, illuminating for effective action on behalf of justice:

In the face of such widely varying situations it is difficult for us to utter a unified message and to put forward a solution which has universal validity. Such is not our ambition, nor is it our mission. It is up to the Christian communities to analyze with objectivity the situation which is proper to their own country, to shed on it the light of the Gospel's unalterable words, and to draw principles of reflection, norms of judgment, and directives for action from the social teaching of the Church. This social teaching has been worked out in the course of history. . . . It is up to these Christian communities, with the help of the Holy Spirit, in communion with the bishops who hold responsibility, and in dialogue with other Christian brethren and all men and women of goodwill, to discern the options and commitments which are called for in order to bring about the social, political, and economic changes seen in many cases to be urgently needed. In this search for the changes which must be promoted, Christians must first of all renew their confidence in the forcefulness and special character of the demands made by the Gospel.[44]

"The process," notes a perceptive interpreter, "is not application of ahistorical principles to situations, but dialogical discernment for action, emerging from concrete situations and the Christian traditions. . . . Social teaching itself is historically constituted via a dialogical development in Christian communities between the resources of their traditions and their specific situation prior to discernment for action."[45]

Our postimmigrant Catholicism has not heard the 1971 Synod of [Catholic] Bishops declare that the vindication of justice and participation in the process of transforming the world is "a constitutive dimension of the preaching of the gospel,"[46] has not heard the 1974 Synod of Bishops proclaim that the Church "believes firmly that the promotion of human rights is required by the gospel and is central to her ministry."[47] In fact, the synod of 1971 confirmed a basic Christian reality: Christian love of neighbor and doing justice are one.[48] "For those of us raised to consider justice a legal matter while the gospel was about 'loving God and neighbor,' the bishops surprised us: 'Christian love of neighbor and justice cannot be separated' [34]."[49]

Our postimmigrant Catholicism has not heard Pope John Paul II argue, in his 1981 encyclical *Laborem exercens (On Human Work),* that in their labor human persons image their Creator and share God's creative action, a source of profound spirituality. It has not listened to his 1987 encyclical *Sollicitudo rei socialis (On Social Concern),* where he states boldly that "the Church's social doctrine adopts a critical attitude toward both liberal capitalism and Marxist collectivism," because both concepts of the development of individuals and peoples are "imperfect and in need of radical correction."[50] It has paid little or no attention to his 1991 encyclical *Centesimus annus (The Hundredth Year)*, where he grants that "the free market is the most efficient instrument for utilizing resources and effectively responding to needs," but insists that "there are many human needs which find no place on the market," that even prior to the logic of a fair exchange of goods there exists something which is due to man and woman because they are human persons.[51]

I think it fair to say that the primary arguments of John Paul's predecessors stemmed from natural law, from reason, from philosophy, from ethics. Fascinating to me is the extent to which John Paul II, profound philosopher by early profession, interweaves Scripture and theological argumentation with natural reason in fashioning his social doctrine. For example, the fifth section (nos. 35–40) of the encyclical *On Social Concern* is headed "A Theological Reading of Modern Problems." The methodology is deliberate, as evidenced by the pontiff's clear declaration. Limiting his analysis of underdevelopment simply to its economic and political causes, and restricting the resources available for true development to the scientific, technical, and political, could not be justified in a pastoral document. There are moral causes, the behavior of persons, and so the decisions must be primarily moral: "For believers, and especially for Christians, these decisions will take their inspiration from the principles of faith, with the help of divine grace."[52]

On the other hand, it is only fair to note that a recent study claims that John Paul II is reversing the earlier emerging articulation of a historically conscious methodology in the Church's social teaching in preference for a transcendental personalism as the basis for universal norms. The Franciscan professor Mary Elsbernd finds in the last two decades of magisterial teaching a significant reinterpretation of Paul VI's *Octogesima adveniens:*

> First, in considering the question, who participates in the development of Catholic social teaching, a shift occurred from the local Christian community to the magisterium alone. Second, with regard to the starting point, a shift occurred from analysis of the local situation to permanent principles of Catholic social doctrine. Third, in considering the contribution of history, a shift occurred from history as a constitutive dimension of social

teaching to an awareness of historical contingencies in the application of social teaching. Fourth, with regard to the place of the gospel, a shift occurred from the gospel as an active partner along with social teaching in dialogue with the signs of the times to the gospel as a primary, distant source of social doctrine. Fifth, the principles of reflection, norms, and directives for action drawn from social doctrine became the content of social doctrine. Thus the three stages are no longer aspects of a method used by local communities. Sixth, once the principles, norms, and directives became identified with social doctrine, the role of the local Christian community shifted from participation in the actual development of social teaching to mere application of permanently valid principles determined by the magisterium. Seventh, there is consequently a shift from Paul VI's claim that a unified message and a universal solution is neither the papal ambition nor its mission.

Finally, with regard to the relationship of Church and world, a shift took place from an ecclesiology which saw the Church as a pilgrim people in the world to an ecclesiology of the Church as the guardian of truth which it dispenses to the world. We argue, however, that both of these ecclesiological dimensions are needed as a kind of ongoing self-corrective mechanism.[53]

Elsbernd argues that recent Catholic social teaching is not characterized by participation and therefore is in peril of losing its credibility. Furthermore, she is convinced that certain inadequacies are inherent in the claim of an ahistorical, universal, permanent social doctrine: It cannot address contemporary unity and diversity; it is unable to make sense of change; it downplays the power of social, political, religious, and economic structures and movements to shape lives and meaning; and practically it ignores the Incarnation.[54]

Principles of Catholic Social Teaching

From the tradition, especially but not completely comprised in official documents, what principles of Catholic social teaching emerge as basic to Christian living? Understandably, these principles have been refined over time, clarified and/or modified by "signs of the times," and they vary in their application to new needs, differing circumstances. Still, six broad principles merit explicit mention.

First, the center of Catholicism's social teaching is the life, dignity, and rights of the human person. The 1974 Synod of Catholic Bishops made this pellucidly clear in a significant statement on "Human Rights and Reconciliation." Said the bishops in common: "Human dignity is rooted in the image and reflection of God in each of us. It is this which makes all persons essentially equal. The integral development of persons makes more clear the divine image in them. In our time the Church has grown more deeply aware of this truth; hence she believes firmly that the promotion of human rights is required by the gospel and is central to her ministry."[55] From this basic dignity that highlights the very first chapter of Scripture (Gen 1:26–27) flow not only the right to life but related rights necessary for each one's integral development as a person: work, food, respect, and so on.

Granted, Old Testament scholars are not at peace in spelling out the content of this correspondence between Elohim and Everyman, between God and the human person. Does the divine image lie in human sovereignty over the nonhuman? Is it that the human mirrors God by being male and female? Is it that, just as ancient kings erected "images" of themselves in subject territory, so humans are God's representatives, to be honored somewhat as God is honored? Is it human consciousness, which images in some fashion the supreme consciousness with whom man and woman can dialogue, creatures analogous to God with whom God can speak and who will hear God's word? Given the Hebrew reluctance to carve the human composite into parts, is there anything in the Genesis text that justifies the later insistence on the "spiritual," on rationality and freedom? Is it not likely that the writer had no definite idea about the content or location of the image?

I continue to sense that Genesis has not betrayed its image secret, even to the most refined instruments of German exegesis. Scholars have wrestled with the text unto frustration, polemicists have exploited it beyond recognition. Yet there it stands, its fundamental affirmation a crucial challenge to any religious anthropology: each human person, male or female, in his or her empiric wholeness, stands in a special relationship to the creating God, a unique relationship that privileges humanity vis-à-vis the nonhuman, a relationship so intimate that we are said to be "like" God. This is basic to any specifically Catholic position on human rights, on male and female dignity.

Second, God's human images have not only rights but responsibilities. There is a peril that lurks in the centrality allotted to the rights of the human person, especially in an age like ours where an understandable clamor for human rights threatens to drown out the less attractive warning about responsibilities. It shows itself, for example, in the thesis that, because my body is mine and no one else's, I have the unchallengeable right to do what I want with that body—from abortion through alcoholism to euthanasia. My body, my money, my turf, "mine and thine," what Augustine of Hippo and John Chrysostom called "those ice-cold words."

Catholic doctrine speaks most integrally when it insistently pairs rights and responsibilities. For our God shaped us not as independent monads but to live together, as one human family, a community. Rugged individualism, where the race is to the shrewd and the swift and the savage, where in the last analysis my sole responsibility is to myself, destroys community, dis-members the family. Biblical justice, the core of God's demands on a covenant people, is fidelity to relationships: responsibilities to God, to my sisters and brothers, to the earth that nourishes me so generously. These responsibilities are mind-boggling; for they demand that we love God above all else, in and through all else; that we love our fellow humans (enemies included) like other selves, love them as Jesus has loved us; that we cherish every facet of God's creation, from rich earth to giant redwood, from the microscopic amoeba to the prowling panther to the shooting star, as a precious gift.

Third, the heart and soul of community is the family: traditionally, father, mother, and children (where situations demand, the one-parent family). Catholicism has never wavered in visualizing such a family as the basic building block of civilizations and cultures, as the primordial natural community, as the church in miniature. Beginning in the fourth century (when Christianity was legalized in the Roman Empire) and maturing around the ninth century, "Christian teachings altered the legal underpinnings of the household and made normative the form of social organization in which husband, wife, and children were responsible to each other for survival, the fulfillment of obligations, mutual love and respect." [56] In consequence, the family deserves special protection, particularly in an age when the traditional family structure is threatened; in an America where half the marriages break up and single-parent families are mushrooming; in a climate where increasingly people are questioning whether anyone can realistically say "for ever." Protective measures must include (but most often do not) the rights of the unborn, of children, of the aging, the right to work, to a family wage, to decent housing, to education.

Fourth, a preferential option for the poor, the disadvantaged, the forgotten. I shall speak of this option in greater detail in my third chapter, on the Cry of the Poor. Here let it suffice to note that the biblical preference for the poor does not imply that they are necessarily holier on a spiritual standard, more deserving from an ethical standpoint. They are "preferred" because they stand in greater need, and therefore have a higher claim on our support. This is the way our God comes through to us in the pages of God's own Book. This is what the God of the Prior Testament demanded of the kings who served God's people. This is what Jesus preached in his preference for the sinner and the sufferer, the outcast and the oppressed. This is what the Fathers of the Church proclaimed in season and out, to powerful princes and powerless people. The expression may be recent; the reality is as ancient as the Exodus.

Fifth, solidarity. For, "if interdependence is an accurate description of our modern world, then solidarity is the appropriate Christian response to this reality."[57] In the context of God's creative intent, we humans are called to overcome barriers of race and religion, of ethnicity and gender, of economic status and nationality. And within Christianity itself, we "are all one in Christ Jesus" (Gal 3:28). We are one body, and within this body no one dare say to any other, "I have no need of you" (1 Cor 12:21). From the nuclear family to the Christian body to the human community, we are called by our one God to live together, to work together, to support one another, to love one another—and this in cultures with more colors and smells, more beliefs and doubts, more tongues and prejudices than Jesus ever experienced.

In his encyclical *On Social Concern,* John Paul II spoke of interdependence as "a moral category" to which "the correlative response, as a moral and social attitude, as a 'virtue,' is solidarity. This then is not a feeling of vague compassion or shallow distress at the misfortunes of so many people, both near and far. On the contrary, it is a firm and persevering determination to commit oneself to the common good, that is to say to the good of all and of each individual, because we are all really responsible for all."[58]

Care for the Earth

The sixth principle, for sheer age and emphasis, is something of a new-comer on the scene: care for God's nonhuman creation, concern for nature. In consequence, I shall allot significantly greater space to this principle than to the richly traditional preceding five.

In my first chapter I noted that ecologists have laid shameful blame for our environmental crises on a Christian interpretation of Genesis 1:28. I noted, too, that God's command to "subdue" and "have dominion" is actually not a license to despotic subjugation; it is a call to reverential care. But it is not only biblicists who have been somewhat late in stressing the intimate, indispensable relationship between nature and humankind as evidenced in their own field of specialization. Official documents, whether universal or regional, have rarely given significant attention to the "things" of God, save (justifiably) to condemn their misuse.[59] And only in recent decades have theologians made profound efforts to shape systematic foundations for ecological theology, to make a theology of the environment an integral facet of the search for justice, for community.

Why such a magisterial and theological lag? One explanation has intrigued me for more than a quarter-century. The Lutheran theologian Joseph Sittler insisted that our basic ecological error is that we Christians have separated creation and redemption. The reason why we can worship nature in Vermont and at the same time manipulate nature in New York is that, in our view, the redemption wrought by Christ leaves untouched the creation wrought by God. And once we wrench redemption from creation, once we put nature out there and grace in here, as long as we omit from our theology of grace humans' transaction with nature, it is irrelevant to Christians whether we reverence the earth or ravish it.[60]

Fortunately, the past several decades have witnessed an ecological awakening within Catholicism. As so often in history, the breakthrough, the impetus, came not from official documents but from the agonizing insights of theologians. A handful of examples must suffice.

First, two influential women. For feminist theologians have been emphasizing, on the one hand, the connection between patriarchal culture, the technological dream of progress, and the environmental crisis, and on the other hand, an idolatrously one-sided masculine idea of God. As early as

1975 Rosemary Ruether linked the ecological movement with the feminist: "Women must see that there can be no liberation for them and no solution to the ecological crisis within a society whose fundamental model of relationships continues to be one of domination." [61] Sally McFague, in a more recent and equally important work, argues that a more maternal imaging of God, along with a careful conception of the world as God's body, could have wholesome implications for understanding our relation to nature.[62]

Thomas Berry, a Passionist priest, has long argued that we are on the brink of an ecological age that can occasion a major revolution in culture and theology. As he put it so simply and yet so profoundly, if we lose the environment, we lose God. He asked us to imagine what our religions would be like, sacramentally speaking, if our abode were something like the lunar landscape. For our symbols and sacraments have been derived directly or indirectly from the natural world. Erode or destroy the natural basis of our religious symbolism, and religion could no longer perform its God-given task.[63] Among his twelve principles for understanding the universe and the role of the human in the universe process, these three have centered the ecological issue for me more powerfully than any other:

> 2. The universe is a unity, an interacting and genetically-related community of beings bound together in an inseparable relationship in space and time. The unity of the planet earth is especially clear; each being of the planet is profoundly implicated in the existence and functioning of every other being of the planet.
>
> 7. The earth, within the solar system, is a self-emergent, self-propagating, self-nourishing, self-educating, self-governing, self-healing, self-fulfilling community. All particular life systems in their being, their sexuality, their nourishment, their education, their governing, their healing, their fulfillment, must integrate their functioning within this larger complex of mutually dependent earth systems.
>
> 12. The main human task of the immediate future is to assist in activating the inter-communion of all the living and non-living components of the earth community in what can be considered the emerging ecological period of earth development.[64]

More recently, the Irish Augustinian Gabriel Daly has set himself "to consider the theological situation that is revealed almost as a by-product of the ecological crisis. We have recently become aware that the Christian theology of creation has been seriously neglected and underdeveloped, especially in the West." Daly is convinced that "creation is not a mere backdrop to redemption but taken into a process that is continuously both creative and redemptive."[65]

Certain directions in Western theology centuries ago, Daly claims, diverted attention from creation and nature. He singles out two preoccupations: (1) with divine transcendence, immutability, and impassibility; (2) with history as a framework for soteriology. First, the difference in kind between God and all that is not God, he insists, "acts as a chasm preventing the affirmation of ontological continuity between God and the cosmos."[66] Even the doctrine of the analogy of being hardly tempers the emphasis on God's "differentness." Any relationship with God is said to be "real" only in the creature. Second, the Protestant "turn to history" as the area of divine revelation and salvation meant that only in history could the Word of God speak to sinful humans. Nineteenth-century liberal Protestantism tended to see nature as a force hostile to us humans, who must achieve our destiny by conquering nature. The approach was summed up by Wilhelm Hermann: "We can no longer hope to find God by seeking him in nature. God is hidden from us in nature. . . . It is only out of life in history that God can come to meet us." For mainline Catholicism, Daly believes, the decisive turn to history came only at and after Vatican II, with its shift from essentialism to historical consciousness.

> But it did nothing for the theology of creation. In point of fact Catholic theology, in opening itself to personal, historical, and existentialist modes of thinking, was thereby embracing a fairly luxuriant anthropocentrism. The time has now come to forge a theological anthropology that will place our human species firmly within its natural matrix and therefore recognize that men and women are not the only beneficiaries of God's attention and loving care.[67]

Daly approaches the relation between creation and redemption by taking them as coextensive and mutually interacting. For want of space, let me simply mention here two themes that are crucial to his reflections: the implications of cosmology for our understanding of God as creator and the implications of evolution for a soteriology that relates closely to nature as creation.

For me personally, at once the most thought-provoking and inspirational single volume by a theologian has been John F. Haught's *The Promise of Nature*. This highly respected Georgetown University theologian believes that process theology comes closer than any other theological alternative "to giving us a framework within which to pull together the insights of science and religion into a cosmology that encourages in us an evolutionary adventurousness as well as a preservative care that might inspire appropriate ethical attitudes toward nature." With the help of science, we can see religious searching as "expressive of the adventurous nature of the universe itself," need not "feel 'lost in the cosmos' in order to embrace the homelessness that religion requires." Religion's essential role in the earth's ecology will take shape primarily in our "unembarrassed cultivation of its inherent sacramentalism and the genuine reverence toward nature that this implies" —a sacramentalism that needs to be nourished by mysticism, silence, and action. Add two challenging statements in the face of traditional theologies: (1) What happens to the cosmos, somehow happens to God. (2) Death sets the person "free from its limited relationship with a proximate terrestrial environment in order to allow a less restricted relationship to the entire cosmos." Here Haught has compelled me to probe ever more deeply into the person (the human as well as the divine) not primarily as an independently conscious substance but as essentially *relational*. "Personality means the capacity for continually intensifying the depth and breadth of relationship to other persons, nature and God." [68] To read Haught on personal immortality requires deep and frequent breathing.

The earth, nature, things, the nonhuman have commonly entered documents of the Catholic magisterium in their relation to the development and progress of man and woman. Take the Second Vatican Council when it urges Christians, while on pilgrimage to a heavenly city, to construct a more human world:

> For when, by the work of their hands or with the aid of technology, man and woman develop the earth so that it may bear fruit and become a dwelling worthy of the whole human family, and when they consciously take part in the life of social groups, they are carrying out God's design, manifested at the beginning of time, that they subdue the earth and bring creation to perfection; and they are developing themselves.[69]

But John Paul II has carried ecology beyond Vatican II, beyond his predecessors. For in his message for the World Day of Peace, January 1, 1990,

"Peace with God the Creator, Peace with All of Creation," he set the ecological crisis within the broader context of the search for peace within society. He linked two principles essential for a solution to the ecological crisis, for a peaceful society: an ordered universe and a common heritage: "Theology, philosophy and science all speak of a harmonious universe, of a 'cosmos' endowed with *its own integrity.* . . . On the other hand, the earth is ultimately a common heritage, the fruits of which are *for the benefit of all.*"[70] He insisted that the Christian vision is grounded in religious convictions stemming from revelation: not only the story of creation and the sin that resulted in earth's rebellion against the human, but a subjugated earth's mysterious yearning for liberation with all God's children (Rom 8: 21–23)—all things made new in Christ (Rev 21:5).

As John Paul saw it, the solution to so profound a moral problem calls for responsibility: a new solidarity between developing nations and the highly industrialized; a world's address to the structural forms of poverty, to exhaustion of the soil, to uncontrolled deforestation; a serious look at lifestyles, consumerism, instant gratification. John Paul called for contemplation of nature's beauty, recognition of its restorative power for the human heart. He made bold to assert that Christians must "realize that their responsibility within creation and their duty toward nature and the Creator are an essential part of their faith."[71] In conclusion he commended to our imitation St. Francis of Assisi, who loved all of God's creatures— not only the poor but animals and plants, natural forces, even Brother Sun and Sister Moon.

Specification of the Principles

Now these principles, indispensable though they are, demand to be concretized in different ages, specified for different times. Such specification harmonizes with the definition of tradition I offered earlier: the best of the past, infused with the insights of the present, with a view to a richer future. Infused with the insights of the present. The Jesuit economist William J. Byron, formerly president of Scranton University and the Catholic University of America, has made this very effort in brief but impressive fashion.[72] He believes that the overarching social question will always be: how can the human community of persons and nations live together in peace secured by justice? This subdivides, for Byron, into seven applications:

religious concerns, political life, family life, economic activities, cultural life, the uses of science and technology, and leisure or recreation. A word on each.

In the area of religious concerns, Byron frames the social question in terms of violence:

> Religious misunderstanding lies at the root of much of the violence in our world. Religion's failure to communicate effectively a moral vision of respect for life also results in widespread toleration of violence in countless forms among persons who claim to have strong religious commitments. Moreover, the presence of the so-called "just war" theory in our religious tradition compels us now not only to reexamine the theory in light of the technology of modern warfare, but also to consider adaptations and applications of the theory to conditions of violence in everyday life.[73]

In the political area, the pressing social-political question would be the need to find an effective international device for settling international differences. It is the question targeted by John Paul II in *Centesimus annus.*

In family life, the bedrock of societal stability, the overriding question is how to prop up the interpersonal commitments that make for permanence in marriage and so create a stable familial existence. Byron insists that changes in society's understanding of family, of household relationships, should not mean a change in the Church's understanding.

The economic category is particularly challenging when it comes to formulating the social question. The issue of top priority should be the elimination of poverty, how to close the gaps between rich and poor around the world. Other economic issues include population concerns, overemphasis on economic success, excessive individualism, unfair compensation policies and practices, inequitable opportunities for education, unemployment, the environmental crisis, and the materialism in the market place that accelerates the loss of a sense of community.

In the cultural category (culture in Bernard Lonergan's definition, "a set of meanings and values informing a common way of life") *the* issue at this time may well be not racism but the rights and dignity of women in contemporary society. Here the attempt must be made to state the very question correctly, with social, anthropological, historical, and theological precision, so that a timely response from Catholic social doctrine may be feasible. What is the meaning of woman in any society? Why is her value an issue today? Where is the balance in asserting rights and assuming duties? Under the uses of science and technology, the predominant social issue would seem to be healthcare (though others may file this question under the economic or political or cultural). Significant, too, is the problem of ethical controls on the uses of science and technology.

Recreation or leisure activity demands uncommon attention. How is leisure time used? Not a question of censorship but of creativity; human dignity versus dehumanizing recreation. This is a basic issue of human personhood.[74]

Preaching the Tradition

My second primary question: how, by all that is good and holy, can Christians preach a tradition? Not by lengthy quotations from official documents. Such documents, for all their value as source and resource, have their own rhetoric. The curial style is not pulpit proclamation. What then? First and above all, I must make the best of the tradition my own. What makes it possible for me to preach with the passion of an Augustine or a Chrysostom, of a Bushnell or a Rauschenbusch, of Vatican II or John Paul II? If I have been captured by the gospel message they preach. Not indeed every jot or tittle of their understanding; for not every Christian idea is carved in Christian stone; ideas develop, are corrected, are refined. The Church grows, not merely in population, but in accuracy and depth of understanding. The primary requisite, therefore? Be filled with the gospel message the tradition reflects and develops, with the Christian substance. Not simply a head trip. I must let the message pulse through my flesh, put fire in my belly. For if I mount the pulpit or approach the podium with a head full of gospel tradition, with a presentation distinguished for Cartesian clarity, but am not aflame with the message, I limp along on one leg. I may instruct, but I will not inspire; I may pontificate, but I will not persuade. An encyclical is not a homily. The homily calls for a response. And the response is not "I believe that God created man and woman in God's own likeness." The response, always and everywhere, must be St. Paul's "What do you want me to do, Lord?" That calls for all the arts of persuasion; it calls for imagination and passion; it calls for vision and fire.

Substantive Facets

On fire, what specifically should I preach, what in the tradition should every Christian proclaim? First, like the earliest Christian preachers, we have the radical task of transforming the less admirable among the dominant values of our society, values shared by all too many Christians of just about every denomination, every religious community. You need not be a Roman Catholic to believe in your heart and proclaim from your housetop what Vatican II declared: "A person is more precious for what he or she is than for what he or she has."[75] It is a dreadfully submerged value: the importance of being over having. You need not be a subject of John Paul II to agree with him when he sets side by side with the anguish and miseries of underdevelopment a contemporary superdevelopment that

> makes people slaves of "possession" and of immediate gratification, with no other horizon than the multiplication or continual replacement of the things already owned with others still better. This is the so-called civilization of "consumption" or "consumerism," which involves so much "throwing-away" and "waste." . . . To "have" objects and goods does not in itself perfect the human subject, unless it contributes to the maturing and enrichment of that subject's "being," that is to say unless it contributes to the realization of the human vocation as such.[76]

Hand in hand with this value, being over having, we must proclaim a related value, sharing rather than possessing. It is relatively easy, minimally perilous, to preach the right to private property, my home as my inviolable castle, my gun as my constitutionally guaranteed safeguard, my hard-earned wages as genuinely mine. It is extremely unsettling when a preacher analyzes that momentous monosyllable "mine," proclaims that the fruit of your toil, what flows from your initiative and your sweat, the money you have amassed and the power you have purchased, your ideas and your computer, all this is your very own only in a limited sense. Extremely unsettling when a preacher proclaims that private property is indeed a right but not an absolute, is subordinate to core personal rights: the right to life, to human dignity, to bodily integrity; proclaims that as for America, so for us Americans, we are not entitled to keep or consume everything we can produce or purchase. For it is through the things of earth, from water to atomic energy, that a man or woman becomes human or inhuman; it is largely by their use of God's creation that our sisters and brothers are saved or damned. And so it should be frightening to realize that at least a billion human persons fall asleep hungry each night, frightening that, despite the dollars pouring into Latin America, despite the wealth of the richest nation on earth, the rich get richer and the poor get poorer.

The tradition I must preach declares that each man, each woman, each child has a strict right to as much of this earth's resources as they need to live a human existence in union with God. All of us must proclaim that, paradoxically, I cannot simply do what I will with what is my own. As a Christian, I may not squander what is my own, even clutch it possessively, in disregard of my brothers and sisters. Whatever I touch, whatever comes within my grasp, I hold in trust from God for the images of God. What I must preach, what all of us must proclaim, is what a thrilling verse from the First Letter of Peter implies: all Christians should employ (literally, "deacon") the many-splendored charisms they have from God for the advantage of one another, "as good stewards of God's dappled grace" (1 Pet 4:10).

But to realize this, we must proclaim with the earliest Christians a conversion of mind and heart. Conversion is, literally, a turning, even a turning round. Within a Christian context, it is a turning to Christ, either for the first time or in a fresh way. But to act as if in all that I do, in all that I have, I manage what is someone else's, what is God's—this does not come easily, naturally. It is a grace . . . and grace is a gift of God that calls for our cooperation (itself a gift). For most of us, it means a new way of looking at a creating God who has a preference for the poor and the sinful; at every human being, however repulsive, as God's image on earth; at each "thing" I see or touch or smell as a vestige of divinity on earth, a trace of God.

A trace of God. You see, God realized that what God is could never be repeated. But God also realized that what God is could be faintly recaptured. God saw that the visible could image the Invisible, that a whirlwind could reflect God's power, a mountain mirror God's majesty, surging waves God's irresistibleness, a star-flecked sky God's breathtaking loveliness. God saw that God's perfection could be imprisoned in something imperfect.

And so, when God gave earth its beginning, God was but painting God's own features on the canvas of a world. And there the God of power was powerless. God could fashion anything a divine mind imagined: ocean or rivulet, rain or rainbow, forest primeval or Milky Way. Yet God could fashion nothing unless it mirrored some perfection of God's. There is no peony that does not speak of God. And if we miss its message, it is not because we know so little of the peony; it is rather that we know so little of God. Ignatius of Loyola caught up in ecstasy as he eyed the sky at night, Teresa of Avila ravished by a rose—these mystics were not simply captivated by material things. They were indeed captivated by sky and rose, but not sheerly that; they had caught for a shattering instant, in a breathless moment, a glimpse of what God must be like. Their ecstasy simply echoes the song of the Psalmist:

> The heavens are telling the glory of God,
>   and the firmament proclaims God's handiwork.
> Day to day pours forth speech,
>   and night to night declares knowledge.
> There is no speech, nor are there words;
>   their voice is not heard;
> yet their voice goes out through all the earth,
>   and their words to the end of the world. (Ps 19:1–4) [77]

To promote such a conversion of heart, we must proclaim, third, the real presence of Christ in the unfortunate and underprivileged, in the impoverished and imprisoned, in the maimed and marginalized. I mean, insist that Christ identifies in a special way with them. Not because they are necessarily holier, but because their need is greater. We must preach, in season and out, the challenging question and answer in Matthew 25: "Lord, when was it that we saw you hungry and gave you food, or thirsty and gave you something to drink? And when was it that we saw you a stranger and welcomed you, or naked and gave you clothing? And when was it that we saw you sick or in prison and visited you?" His answer? "Truly I tell you, insofar as you did it to one of the least of these my brothers and sisters, you did it to me" (vv. 37–40).

Unless our believing brothers and sisters are captured by this vision, unless this is intrinsic to their spirituality, sharing rather than possessing will be at best an act of charity, not the biblical justice which is a relationship of responsibility that stems from our covenant with Christ. But if the faithful before us are to see Christ in the most unlikely of men and women, we who proclaim Matthew 25 must be seared by it. That conviction must tremble on our lips; it should shape not simply our soup kitchens but our gospel proclamation as well.

To implement such a profoundly Christian spirituality, we must proclaim, fourth, the reality that binds us to all that is human. I mean what we call "community." Throughout history, in times of crisis, the temptation that draws man and woman is isolationism. Whether it's war in Europe or a Great Depression, whether it's crime on our streets or division in our religions, the tendency is to bolt our doors, man the barricades, huddle together in our safe little groups. The genuinely Christian reaction contradicts all that. Our community expands in ever-widening concentric circles. We begin with the local community; call it parish or whatever. This expands to the larger set of communities sometimes called a diocese. The diocese expands out to the church universal. And the church universal spreads its arms out to the whole of humanity. For ultimately our parish is the human family.

A pungent question, for the preacher and the congregation: Can I honestly declare, with St. Paul, that no one of us Christians can say to any other, "I have no need of you" (1 Cor 12:21)? Dare I expand the Pauline context and declare that no human, Christian or Jew, Muslim or Buddhist, agnostic or utter unbeliever, can say to any other, "I have no need of you"? It is simply Frederick Buechner's spider web: touch the web, touch humanity, at any point, for good or evil, and the whole web trembles, the whole of humanity quivers. Do you believe that?

General Principles or Concrete Issues?

Preaching the tradition is relatively easy when the tradition is long established and quite broad in its formulation: the right to life, to human dignity, to bodily integrity, to a living wage, to freedom from discrimination on the basis of race or religion or gender. But how concrete dare I get? How preach a justice issue when the issue is fairly new, a tradition not yet in place, a problem bitterly contested by good Christians—when I must draw my own conclusions from Scripture and the broader tradition? Do I preach affirmative action, equal pay for equal work irrespective of gender, nutrition and hydration for irreversible coma, gays in the military, protests at abortion clinics, boycotting a brutal Stallone or Schwarzenegger celluloid? Should California priests rage against Proposition 187 (now passed) limiting drastically the state's benefits to undocumented aliens, illegal immigrants? Do I preach against discrimination on the basis of sexual orientation?

Some Christians insist that the pulpit must limit itself to general principles. Teach simply what Jesus taught and parishioners will make the right decisions in the moral order. I cannot agree. Homilies that avoid concrete applications risk saying nothing. If I mount the pulpit with "Scripture alone" in my hands, if I limit my preaching to the broad biblical imperatives, if I simply repeat scriptural slogans like "Man and woman do not live on bread alone," "My peace I give to you," "Seek first the kingdom of God," "Love your neighbor as yourself," "Wives, be subject to your husbands," hungry stomachs will stay bloated, the arms race will escalate, dissidents will rot in political prisons, blacks will return to their slavery, and women will continue to be second-class citizens in much of the world. If I preach only the traditions that have age and universality behind them, if I make no effort to touch the tradition to fresh issues, I risk betraying my prophetic calling, even rejecting incarnational theology.

No, the gospel must be touched to concrete human living. The Church grows—the whole Church, prelates and priests, ministers of all denominations, laymen and laywomen, all the baptized—in its understanding of what the gospel demands. It is this fresh understanding that must be preached—what the perennial gospel, the living tradition, demands or suggests in the context of our time and space. But the neuralgic problem remains: how concrete dare I get?

First, some bad news. There is no simple solution, no all-purpose push button to activate answers to injustice. Most issues call for discussion, discernment, prayer; some call for blood, sweat, and tears. Of course, I can proclaim today what the United Nations World Food Conference declared in 1974: "every man, woman, and child has the inalienable right to freedom from hunger and malnutrition. . . ." But the causes are confoundingly complex. Is nature the villain—"acts of God"? Is it people—the world growing too fast? Is it productivity—lack of agricultural know-how? Is it our international economic order—a whole web of unjust relationships between rich and poor countries? Experts, men and women of good will, disagree.

Moreover, it is not the task of Christian preachers to solve complex social, political, and economic issues in a sermon. Our task is to raise consciousness, help our people to become aware of issues, sensitive to injustice. My function is to present biblical justice, Christian tradition, and contemporary agonies so effectively that the faithful in a parish will gather to ask three questions: (1) What are the justice issues in our parish, in our area? (2) What resources do we command to attack these issues? (3) What, in the concrete, shall we do?

Where, for the preacher, is the good news? I do not believe we can bar the controversial from Christian proclamation simply because it is controversial. After all, I must move the gospel to this age, this country, this community; but the meaning and demands of the gospel today are chock-full of complexity. And the more complex an issue, the more open to controversy.

Granted, the pulpit is not the proper forum in which to pontificate on complicated, controverted political and socioeconomic issues. But here the crucial word is "pontificate." On such issues, in a short span of time, with no room for counterargument, I dare not speak in dogmatic fashion, as if I alone am the trumpet of the Lord.[78] But if I dare not dogmatize, I may still raise the issues, lay them out, even tell my people where I stand and why. Not to impose my convictions as gospel, but to quicken their Christian conscience, spur them to personal reflection.

Indeed I must avoid taking unfair advantage of a captive audience, especially since the expertise in the pews often exceeds my own. Inasmuch as the suffering faithful, however sorely provoked, are expected by immemorial custom to hold their tongues as I empty my quiver against what I see as political assault on our children or racial discrimination in housing, I should provide another forum—parish hall, smaller discussion groups—where controversial issues may be properly debated, where all who wish to speak their piece may be heard, where the consciences I have stirred may be coordinated for effective action. For I must guard against a persistent ministerial peril, where I see the ordained minister as alone bearing the burden of Christian guidance, of pastoral counseling. For myself, a sentence from the Second Vatican Council is remarkably clear, concise, compelling: "Let the laity not imagine that their pastors are always such experts that to every problem which arises, however complicated, they can readily give a concrete solution, or even that such is their mission."[79]

Some years ago a permanent deacon in the Roman Catholic Diocese of

Rockville Center, Long Island, lent me a useful suggestion from his long years in the advertising game. If preaching is to be effective, he noted, especially in troublesome areas of justice that divide a community, we can learn much from the approach of the advertiser—on TV and radio, in newspapers and magazines. Know your audience: what turns them on or off, their hang-ups, their backgrounds and social situations, the influences on their living and thinking. Don't pontificate or browbeat; use all the arts of persuasion, the arts that sell millions each day on products, from diamonds to Doublemint, they never suspected were essential to human living. Remember the insight of Jesus, "The children of this world are shrewder . . . than the children of light" (Lk 16:8).

A final word. A good fifteen years ago I was much moved by Ralph Waldo Emerson's insistence that a preacher's "sermon should be rammed with life." In the midst of a famous iconoclastic address at the Harvard Divinity School on July 15, 1838, he railed at the junior pastor of his grandfather Ripley's church in Concord:

> I once heard a preacher who sorely tempted me to say I would go to church no more. . . . He had lived in vain. He had no one word intimating that he had laughed or wept, was married or in love, had been commended, or cheated, or chagrined. If he had ever lived or acted, we were none the wiser for it. The capital secret of his profession, namely, to convert life into truth, he had not learned. Not one fact in all his experience, had he yet imported into his doctrine. . . . Not a line did he draw out of real history. The true preacher can always be known by this, that he deals out to the people his life,—life passed through the fire of thought.[80]

The justice traditions that stem from the Hebrew prophets and Jesus the Christ, that have been tested and fired, heated and hammered in the forge of Christian history, can indeed transform our preaching. But only on condition that they pass through the fire of our lives. Only if we live the just word we preach. Only if the faithful and the unfaithful alike sense that it is not only *Christ's* body and blood that have been offered for them, but my body and blood as well. Short of that, the just word will be just a word and nothing more.

THREE

Preaching the Cry of the Poor

In the Roman Catholic liturgy the first reading from Scripture is followed by a sung or recited responsorial psalm. One of those psalms contains this response, repeated again and again by the faithful: "The Lord hears the cry of the poor." The Lord does indeed hear the cries of the disadvantaged, those who hunger for bread or love, for freedom or peace, though the "mystery of iniquity" prevents us from understanding just how the Lord "hears" the cries of the crucified images of Christ in the sub-Sahara and Serbia, in Northern Ireland and South Africa, on the icy streets of every American megalopolis. My present problem is not with the Lord, not with God's hidden plan of salvation, not even with the largely insoluble mystery of evil. My problem is: do we who proclaim the gospel hear the cry of the poor?

The Cry of the Poor

First, the cry of the poor. Recall, from Chapter 1, who the poor are in God's inspired Word. Not only the poverty-stricken, but the leper ostracized from society, the widow at the mercy of dishonest judges, orphans with no parents to love them, the adulterous woman to be stoned according to the law of Moses, those of a lower class oppressed by the powerful— even, by extension, wealthy toll-collector Zacchaeus, despised because of his job.[1]

Who are the poor that cry out to us in our time? Let me sketch seven groups. Not that these exhaust the categories of the disadvantaged and disenfranchised, the oppressed and distressed, the despised and discarded. These are simply striking examples.

Children

First, the most vulnerable of all: our children. TV trumpets our love for children, yet one of every five (perhaps every four) little ones grows up hungry in the richest nation on earth; 40,000 each year do not survive to see their first birthday. In one year alone (1990) 407,000 minors were placed in foster homes. We proclaim our young as the flower of the future, yet every twenty-six seconds a child runs away from home, every forty-seven seconds a child is abused or neglected, every seven minutes a boy or girl is arrested for drug abuse, every thirty-six minutes a child is killed or injured by a gun, each day more than 1,400 teenage girls become mothers—two-thirds of them unmarried. We piously dedicate this decade to unparalleled American education, yet uncounted Johnnies still can't read, and every day 135,000 children go to school with a deadly weapon.[2] We live in an America where each day more than 500 children ages ten to fourteen begin using illegal drugs, and more than a thousand start on alcohol. An America where among teens fifteen to nineteen the third-leading cause of death is firearms, and the rate of teenage suicide has tripled in thirty years. An America where each year 1.5 million children are forcibly prevented from ever seeing the light of day. The head of Covenant House, Sister Mary Rose McGeady, dedicated her 1991 book *God's Lost Children* "to the 1,000,000 homeless children who slept on America's streets last year, scared, cold, hungry, alone, and most of all, desperate to find someone who cares."[3]

The most recent report from the United Nations Children's Fund *(The Progress of Nations)* informs us that nine out of ten young people murdered in industrialized countries are killed in the United States. The U.S. poverty rate for children is more than double that of any other major industrialized nation. In the past twenty years, while other industrialized countries were bringing children out of poverty, only the United States and Great Britain slipped backward.[4] Not surprisingly, I recall that in an interview with *Time* magazine Sylvia Hewlett remarked that in the United States there are greater tax benefits for breeding horses than for producing children.

In my own back yard, the District of Columbia, a dismaying trend has recently come to light. Children in Washington are planning their own funerals: how they want to look, how to be dressed, where to be waked. Not out of curiosity, not from a Christian consciousness of death's significance. They simply do not believe they will be around very long, have every reason to expect they will not grow up. Where they play, coke and crack are homicidal kings. Over a period of five years, 224 of their childhood friends died from gunfire. Some were deliberate targets, others just happened to be there, at least one lay in a cradle. And so the living little ones have begun planning for the worst, as if their own murders are inevitable, as if their own dreams will surely be just as cruelly cut short.[5] We live in a "land of the free" where one of every four youngsters is living in some sort of hell.

And across the world? In wars over the last decade, more than 1.5 million children were killed, more than 4 million physically disabled. About 5 million children are now in refugee camps. One hundred million children are living on the streets. Child labor "allows millions of children to knot carpets in India and Pakistan, to harvest bananas in Egypt, to salvage rags in Egypt and to harvest cotton in the Sudan."[6] How many children will die in the 1990s alone, most from diseases we know how to prevent? One hundred and fifty million!

These are not naked statistics. As Marian Wright Edelman, president of the Children's Defense Fund, put it, "poverty steals children's potential and in doing so steals from all of us." Her conservative estimate, on the basis of expert economic advice, is that "future losses to the economy stemming from the effects of *just one year* of child poverty for 14.6 million children reach as high as $177 billion."[7] Even more tragic than the financial effects are the personal consequences: iron deficiency that causes anemia and impairs children's problem solving, motor coordination, attention, concentration, long-term IQ scores; hunger that induces fatigue, dizziness, irritability, headaches, ear infections, weight loss, frequent colds; stunted growth that makes for learning problems; 100,000 American children homeless each day; overcrowded, unsafe, unhealthy, indecent housing, including cockroach, rat, and mouse infestation; fire-prone mobile homes; crime-ridden neighborhoods; inferior schools with fewer financial and material resources, less skilled administrators and teachers; fewer stimulating activities such as family trips and camps, music classes and hobbies; financial barriers to college education; child abuse and neglect; unmarried childbearing; limited access to good jobs; delinquency and violence in later life.[8]

In 1989 the U.N. General Assembly adopted the Convention on the Rights of the Child. By May 1993, it had been ratified by 136 countries; 23 more had signed it but not yet ratified it. Among the 29 countries that have neither signed nor ratified the convention, the United States stands out ingloriously—"which puts us in the company of Iraq, Saudi Arabia and Somalia."[9]

Here I find pertinent and instructive (though not limited to children) what Michael Kinsley had to say early in 1995 about "wedge issues," which "pry voters away from their traditional allegiances":

> Welfare is the classic wedge issue. Conservative welfare reformers may say their primary concern is to liberate the poor from the shackles of their underclass culture, and some of them may even believe it. But only the most naive or cynical among them would deny that the political potency of the welfare issue derives mostly from resentment of the poor as leeches on society, not from sympathy for their plight.[10]

The AIDS-Afflicted

Second, the cry of the AIDS-afflicted. You know, countless Americans who claim to be people of compassion see in AIDS God's own plague on the promiscuous; for all too many, the victims are simply getting from God what they deserve. I myself heard the HIV-cry with Christian ears in 1988 in Nashville. An Anglican minister was addressing the 73d Assembly of the Catholic Health Association of the United States. To an audience that often wept openly Canon William Barcus said: "I stand here with you— as a brother to you, a churchman, a man with AIDS. A man who regrets nothing of the love and goodness he has known, who stops now to notice flowers, children at play. . . . A man who loves his church from his heart, from every molecule in him." In the course of his address Canon Barcus recalled a 1944 photo essay in *Life* magazine:

It was about the red foxes of Holmes County, Ohio, who lived in the woods and ate mostly mice and crickets, but sometimes also chicken and quail. This, the story explained, "made the brave men of Holmes County angry because they wanted to kill the quail themselves." So one Saturday about 600 men and women and their children got together and formed a big circle five miles across. They all carried sticks and started walking through the woods and fields, yelling and baying to frighten the foxes, young and old, out of their holes. Inside this diminishing circle the foxes ran to and fro, tired and frightened. Sometimes a fox would, in its anger, dare to snarl back, and it would be killed on the spot for its temerity. Sometimes one would stop in its anguish and try to lick the hand of its tormentor. It too would be killed.

Sometimes, the photo showed, other foxes would stop and stay with their own wounded and dying. Finally, as the circle came closer together, down to a few yards across, the remaining foxes went to the center and lay down inside, for they knew not what else to do. But the men and the women knew what to do. They hit these dying wounded with their clubs until they were dead, or they showed their children how to do it. This is a true story. *Life* reported and photographed it. It happened for years in Holmes County every weekend. The good Christian people of Holmes County considered it sport and it still goes on.

I stand before you today as one weary of running, as one wounded myself, and I say to the churches, the churches first, and then to the government, the silent government, and then to the world: "What have you done to my people? What have you done to your own people—beautiful people?" . . .

My people are being destroyed, and your people, and all our people together. Not only by an illness called AIDS, but by a darker illness called hatred. . . . The Christ, Jesus, the compassionate lord of life and lord of more forgiveness and lord of more hope is the one we have vowed to follow and be ultimately guided by. We must tell that to our smugly self-righteous brothers and sisters. . . . For if we do not, their souls will perish in the circle of misunderstanding and scorn they teach so many as they club and scream their disdain for the outsider, the misunderstood, the different. . . . Sadly . . . too many with AIDS have wondered if they had any alternative but to go to the center of the circle and lie down and die.

Where are you in that circle? Where are we? Where would Christ be? . . .

For all of us within an awakening church . . . I say to the world, "Help us. Join us." To you as church . . . I say from long despairing peoples of all kinds, "Help us. Please help us. Be the gospel alive!" [11]

Uncounted Christians find it difficult to "be the gospel alive" where Acquired Immune Deficiency Syndrome is the issue. It is indeed an epidemic, and it raises profound moral questions for every institution of American society.[12] Healthcare institutions, for example, must balance a patient's right to privacy and confidentiality against the need to inform others (particularly public-health officials) of the presence of AIDS or exposure to HIV. What obligations may compel physicians to treat AIDS patients, even at risk to their own health? What excuses are legitimate?

Significant questions indeed, these and other moral issues. My question here, while not irrelevant to ethics and morality, goes beyond them. It is again a question of biblical justice, of fidelity to relationships and responsibilities imposed by our covenant with Yahweh or with Christ. Such fidelity calls for a profound change in a widespread attitude that cloaks itself in religion: God is giving the AIDS-afflicted simply what they deserve. The genuinely Christian attitude was summed up by Cardinal Joseph Bernardin of Chicago in a 1986 pastoral letter:

God is loving and compassionate, not vengeful. Made in God's image, every human being is of inestimable worth, and the life of all persons, whatever their sexual orientation, is sacred and their dignity must be respected. . . . The Gospel reveals that while Jesus did not hesitate to proclaim a radical ethic of life grounded in the promise of God's kingdom, he never ceased to reach out to the lowly, to the outcasts, of his time—even if they did not live up to the full demands of his teaching.[13]

The Elderly

Third, the cry of the elderly. What our dominant American culture glorifies is youth, strength, beauty. Old age is rarely mentioned in polite society, at cocktail parties. The ideal of aging? Not to seem to age at all. Bob Hope and Eva Gabor, Ronald Reagan and Mother Teresa, Cary Grant and Grandma Moses, John XXIII and Jacqueline Kennedy, Paul Newman and Katharine Hepburn—here is eternal youth. If after sixty or sixty-five you can continue a productive career, if you can still stroke a tennis ball, straddle a Honda, or satisfy a sexual partner, then your aging is ideal.

Most Americans, however, do not age so gracefully, so creatively, so productively. Most sexagenarians, practically all septuagenarians, are retired. In our culture, to be retired is to be useless: the aged rarely serve a practical purpose; they don't "do" anything. Not only are they irrelevant to big business, big government, big military, big education; they are a drain on the economy. Whether glowing with health or in a permanent vegetative state, they use up medical resources, medical miracles, that could benefit the useful members of society. The "new boys [and girls] on the block," economic man and economic woman, draw their knowledge and wisdom from computers, not from the hoary stories of the aging. Honor them, naturally—till they become an economic liability meriting a merciful injection. Respect for elders, of course; but life in the same house with Grandpa and Grandma? It simply would not work. Too wide a gap between the generations; the old folk are not "with it." On the whole, a nursing home makes better American sense. And there they sit, watching and waiting: watching TV's "Married—with Children" and waiting for someone they carried in their womb to visit and "watch one hour" (Mt 26:40) with them.

It is all so different from many another culture, from attitudes to aging in various religions of the world.[14] Take, for example, the insight of southern Ghana's Akans: knowledge is power, but aging is wisdom—a wisdom that calls for reverence, for respect. The woodland Ojibway of North America reflect the tradition of Native Americans in their insistence, "Honor the aged, in honoring them you have life and wisdom." For Confucians filial piety, respect for elders, is the supreme principle of morality; for it can define the very meaning of our being in this world, is a powerful binding force that produces a stable society, is a source of world peace and order. The Hindu tradition refuses to focus on the physical weakness and disabilities of the elderly, stressing instead their spiritual maturity and wisdom, which command universal respect and reveal them as models of an authentic human life serving all humanity disinterestedly. I hear the Buddha admonishing his followers to treat parents as a living Buddha. Despite areas of poverty, exploitation, and illiteracy, most Buddhists are concerned to take care of their elders with respect and pride. How keen of Buddhists to regard aging as not diminishment but increase, a movement toward fuller life, neither a downward spiral toward dissolution nor a triumphal procession to glory and immortality.

The Hebrew Testament and rabbinic reflection thereon insist that the younger should acknowledge the dignity and worth of the aged somewhat as they receive the presence of God. Such reverence stems from a realization that parents, like God, are creators. They transmit their experience of the past not as sheer knowledge but as a living witness to God's presence. Because life is a gift of God and all moments of life are equally sacred, the period of deterioration in aging demands special concern to preserve life with dignity. "Aging can mean growth, a celebration, the sanctification of time, an opportunity once again for experiencing the presence which makes us truly human," for pursuing righteousness, like Abraham, in imitation of God.[15] All too few of us listen to Rabbi Abraham Joshua Heschel as he appeals so insightfully, so eloquently, so touchingly to contemporary society:

Old men need a vision, not only recreation.
Old men need a dream, not only a memory.
It takes three things to attain a sense of significant being:
God, a soul and a moment.
The three are always here.
Just to be is a blessing, just to live is holy.[16]

"Just to live is holy." How far have we traveled, when patient-assisted suicide threatens to be the response to intolerable pain!

Women

Fourth, the cry of women. We have stopped saying women have no souls, yet we pay them less than men for comparable work, 43 percent of single mothers are poor, and it took us longer to legislate against sexual abuse than to condemn black slavery. The feminist movement cries for "the empowerment of women for the transformation of social and religious structures beyond patriarchy—that model of social organization that assures men, predominantly white men, have control and dominant power within social and religious structures."[17] Women cry that for all too long their voices and their experience have been silent not only in government and industry, in the home and the school, but in the churches and in religious life, in the interpretation of Scripture and the understanding of theology, in every area where ideas are generated that change the world and decisions are made that affect the way women think, the way they live, the way they worship.

Women cry aloud against the "feminization of poverty" in the United States, sometimes termed more accurately the "pauperization of women and children."[18] They cry out against the powerlessness of women to shape the world in any but a masculine mold.[19] They cry out against a division of labor within the family that is gender-based, does not take into consideration a woman's gifts, talents, education, or desires, a division of responsibility that "disenfranchises men from the full potential of their fatherhood while it disenfranchises women from the full potential of their personhood."[20] They cry out against a Catholic education that trains women for the professions yet still holds out as the ideal the full-time mother. They cry out against the multiple demands made on them by the family, the workplace, and the common good, demands that create needless stress, corrosive frustration, even profound guilt.[21] They cry out in one "Women's Creed":

> We look forward to the future in faith and hope, working for the day when we and all our sisters no longer have to fit a stereotype, but are free to use all our gifts and to share in all the benefits of human life and work. We look forward to the age of peace, when violence is banished, both women and men are able to love and to be loved and the work and wealth of our world is justly shared.[22]

The African American

Fifth, the cry of our black sisters and brothers. Their cry echoes the cry of Yahweh to Pharaoh, "Let my people go!" Rather than listen to bald, barren statistics, listen to black Sister Thea Bowman, stricken with breast cancer and bone cancer, racing her wheelchair across the country to spread her gospel of love: "I'm not going to die. I'm going home like a shooting star." Listen to her as she spoke her mind passionately in 1989 to the bishops of the Catholic Church in the United States:

> Despite the civil rights movement of the '60s and the socio-educational gains of the '70s, blacks in the '80s are still struggling, still scratching and

clawing as the old folks said, still trying to find home in the homeland and home in the church, still struggling to gain access to equal opportunity.

A disproportionate number of black people are poor. Poverty, deprivation, stunted physical, intellectual and spiritual growth—I don't need to tell you this, but I want to remind you, more than a third of the black people that live in the United States live in poverty, the kind of poverty that lacks basic necessity.

I'm talking about old people who have worked hard all their lives and don't have money for adequate food or shelter or medical care.

I'm talking about children who can never have equal access and equal opportunity because poverty doomed them to low birth weight and retardation and unequal opportunity for education. . . .

Black children are twice as likely as white children to be born prematurely, to suffer from low birth weight, to live in substandard housing, to have no parent employed. . . .

One of every 21 black males is murdered. A disproportionate number of our men are dying of suicide and AIDS and drug abuse and low self-esteem.[23]

From my limited, mostly secondhand understanding, five realities, at times harrowing, at times heartening, at times harrowing and heartening together, confront the man or woman privileged or presumptuous enough to preach to these particular images of God.

1. The people in question are used to a *struggle for survival.* They have experienced, often still experience, what it means to do without: without food, without education, without work, without wealth, without luxuries. If and when they do come into material goods, most are not spoiled by them. Their struggle puts many of them into the camp of the Hebrew Testament *anawim.* I mean those pious, humble folk, originally the materially poor, oppressed, downtrodden, who were so conscious of their spiritual need, so aware of their dependence, that they looked to the Lord for strength and help, looked to God as their savior. These are the "poor" the prophet Amos had primarily in mind when he threatened God's people with punishment "because they sell the righteous for silver, and the needy for a pair of sandals—they who trample the head of the poor into the dust of the earth, and push the afflicted out of the way" (Amos 2:6-7).

2. The family, for them, is all too often not our current father, mother, and one or two children. It is the *extended family.* There may be thirteen or sixteen in one house—brothers, sisters, kids born out of wedlock. It

frequently includes a woman of forty or so, already a grandmother raising grandchildren. The advantage? Such a family relates intimately to the New Testament, where everybody is a brother or sister. Here there is a bonding, recognition of sisterhood and brotherhood. Disadvantage? It doesn't always work. The culprits? Crack and coke, deadly weapons, imprisonment. But even dysfunctional families know that addiction is a dis-ease, that it destroys relationships.

3. There is an *openness to rescue,* to the power of God. I mean an awareness that Somebody bigger than I has to come in and straighten things out. It gives these people a particular sense of "the real." With this goes a graphic aphorism reported to me by my good friend and colleague Father Raymond Kemp, a long-time pastor of African Americans: "You'd better make a lot of friends on your way up, because you'll need them on your way down." They look at the Donald Trumps and the Michael Jacksons of this world and say, "It won't last." Events will bring the "biggies" down.

4. Intimate to such urban existence is a *sense of healing.* Not so much from doctors and priests or pastors. Rather the expectation that God will bring healing, even that certain diseases may be to their benefit. A person who tested positive for HIV over ten years, for example, had faith that God cares, God heals (even if God doesn't always cure); somehow God will make it come right.

5. *Nihilism.* I mean a pervasive feeling among all so many that there is no future beyond this desperate moment, settling a score, proving yourself a man. And so you have kids killing kids, a life for a Reebok, the lust for the almighty dollar. Much of it stems from poverty, a poverty that causes personal depression. Why work for $5.25 an hour in McDonald's when you can make $500 or $1,000 a week selling or delivering crack? Expensive clothes (the hip-hop culture), rap music—the stress is on today; life is for now. Hence our District of Columbia youngsters preparing their own funerals. On *Donahue,* Father Kemp was asked by a teenager if he would officiate at her funeral!

Here we preachers face not only a crisis of culture; we confront a crisis of faith.

Refugees and the Displaced

A particularly harrowing cry reaches our ears from refugees and the displaced. Refugees—men, women, and children forced by war or persecution to flee their native countries—number conservatively 16,255,000.[24] The internally displaced—forced from their homes to walk their countries' roads to unfamiliar resting places—may exceed 25 million.[25] These dreadfully deprived humans suffer not only the obvious ills: hunger, cold, disease, separation. At this moment our earth is sown with more than one hundred million land mines in more than sixty countries.[26] Because of mines, most of Mozambique's roads are unusable; Cambodia is still a killing field (36,000 casualties at this writing), and half its arable land is unserviceable; Afghanistan lists between 350,000 and 500,000 victims. Angola, with a population of 11 million, hosts between nine and fifteen million mines. A sobering fact: "Most land mines are made in the developed world and sold in the developing world."[27]

It is not generally known that the United States lost 7,300 soldiers to land mines in Vietnam, and that the removal of mines in Kuwait cost us more lives than did Desert Storm itself. The United States Senate has indeed ratified the 1980 United Nations Convention on Conventional Weapons that banned any method or means of combat that cannot be directed at a specific military objective. Apparently because of its ineffectiveness, a review of that convention by all of the original signers has been taking place as I write: two meetings already held in Vienna and Geneva and another scheduled for spring 1996 in Geneva. But, even though President Clinton, in a historic speech to the U.N. General Assembly on September 24, 1994, advocated eventual total elimination of antipersonnel land mines, our government's position in Geneva, put simply, insists only that mines not placed in marked and monitored mine fields must contain a self-destruct mechanism.

Ironically, that position falls far short of what is required under a one-year moratorium that was sponsored by Senator Patrick Leahy (D-Vt.), passed by the Senate in 1996 by a 67-27 vote, and signed into law by President Clinton in late January 1996. The moratorium restricts the use of land mines by U.S. forces to marked and monitored international borders and demilitarized zones. The moratorium will begin after a three-year waiting period designed to give the Pentagon time to develop alternatives to land mines.[28] A U.S. three-year moratorium on export of land mines that was originally to last through October 1996 has been extended through September 1997. At present, no country save France has banned the *production* of land mines. In consequence, 500 men, women, and children will be land-mine casualties each week across the world, innocent victims of power and greed.[29]

I am convinced that the only policy that responds adequately to ethical and biblical justice is a total ban on the production, sale, use, and stockpiling of antipersonnel land mines by every nation across the world.

Death Row

Finally, a group of men and women whose appearance among the "poor" may turn many readers livid. For as I write, America is awash in a new crusade, a nationwide reaction against a frightening escalation of violence. I mean an angry, demanding cry for capital punishment. It stems in large measure, but not entirely, from a twin conviction: (1) that only execution is fit punishment for certain crimes like murder, rape and sexual abuse of children, treason and a Hitlerian butchery of the innocent; and (2) that capital punishment is an effective way to combat the contemporary trend to violence.

My problems with capital punishment are primarily two; each is pertinent within this chapter because each has to do with life. My first problem has been succinctly framed by Manhattan District Attorney Robert M. Morgenthau in an Op-Ed column of the *New York Times:* "Prosecutors must reveal the dirty little secret they too often share only among themselves: The death penalty actually hinders the fight against crime." In summary he declares that "capital punishment is a mirage that distracts society from more fruitful, less facile answers. It exacts a terrible price in dollars, lives and human decency. Rather than tamping down the flames of violence, it fuels them while draining millions of dollars from more promising efforts to restore safety to our lives." [30]

Effectiveness? In 1975, when Morgenthau became district attorney, there were 648 homicides in Manhattan; in 1994 there were 330—a significant reduction, without executions, through more fruitful methods. Cost? A Duke University study in 1993 found that for each person executed in North Carolina, the state paid over $2 million more than it would have cost to imprison the convict for life. In New York the death penalty would cost the state $118 million a year; a fraction of that sum can finance an array of other solutions to crime. Justice? No one disagrees that innocent people have been executed; the only argument is, how many? "A 1987 study in the Stanford Law Review identified 350 cases in this century in which innocent people were wrongly convicted of crimes for which they could have received the death penalty; of that number, perhaps as many as 23 were executed. New York led the list with eight." [31]

Morgenthau's conclusion: Capital punishment is the enemy of law enforcement.

My second argument stems from the sanctity of all human life. Here we touch a dreadfully complex issue. I would be hard put to argue an absolute —that the state never has the right to take a life. I would rather submit that we humans have developed in our humanity to such a point that killing as punishment is unnecessary, that there are more effective ways of preserving the moral order. In our Preaching the Just Word retreat/workshops, John Carr of the U.S. Catholic Conference often points to a strange succession of events: a medical doctor kills a fetus; an antiabortionist kills the doctor; the state kills the antiabortionist. Sheer vengeance, retribution, an eye for an eye. But, a well-known talk-show host asked me, what's wrong with vengeance, with retribution? A legitimate question for ethics and moral theology, even though at first sight it seems to clash with the firm affirmation of the Old Testament and the New, "Vengeance is mine, says the Lord" (Deut 32:35; Rom 12:19). Paradoxically, there is statistical support for the argument that by their brutalizing and dehumanizing effect on society, executions cause more murders than they prevent. After each execution life is held less sacred by the community in question. Violence begets violence.

Although the worldwide trend to abolish the death penalty continues, the United States is hardly part of the movement. A vast majority of our people, perhaps 75 percent (up from less than 50 percent in 1966), support capital punishment. In September 1994 a crime bill was enacted by the Senate and the House, and approved by the president, that expanded the number of crimes subject to the federal death penalty from two to more than sixty. A particularly appalling miscarriage of justice occurred in 1995 in Texas. Jesse DeWayne Jacobs was sentenced to death for a murder to which he had originally confessed. Later he claimed the crime had been committed by his sister. In the subsequent trial of the sister, the prosecutor disavowed the confession he had used to convict Jacobs and argued that Jacobs's sister had pulled the trigger and that he had not anticipated any murder. Still, he was executed. The Supreme Court? Six to three against him.[32]

Opposition to the death penalty is not, strictly speaking, part of the Catholic Church's obligatory doctrine, binding on all the faithful. Still, it is increasingly "a part of the absolute reverence for life that is taught universally by the church."[33] The recent *Catechism of the Catholic Church* stated that, inasmuch as the taking of a life must be the last and only available way to carry out a legitimate need of the state, the death penalty can rarely if ever be morally justified. In 1980 the U.S. Catholic bishops, by a vote of 145 to 31 with 41 abstentions, urged that the death penalty be abolished. Various U.S. episcopal statements argue that the death penalty is an affront to the human dignity of executed and executor alike; that, instead of protecting society, it may even accelerate the cycle of violence; that it makes violence an answer to difficult human problems, the easy way out of addressing complex, pervasive, and expensive problems; that it can only further erode respect for life and increase the brutalization of society; that life is so precious and inviolable that the state must forbid not only abortion and nuclear destruction but capital punishment as well.[34] And most recently, on March 25, 1995, an encyclical of Pope John Paul II addressed this issue in strong language:

> There is a growing tendency, both in the church and in civil society, to demand that [the death penalty] be applied in a very limited way or even that it be abolished completely. The problem must be viewed in the context of a system of penal justice ever more in line with human dignity and thus, in the end, with God's plan for man and society. The primary purpose of the punishment which society inflicts is to "redress the disorder caused by the offense." Public authority must redress the violation of personal and social rights by imposing on the offender an adequate punishment for the crime, as a condition for the offender to regain the exercise of his or her freedom. In this way authority also fulfills the purpose of defending public order and ensuring people's safety, while at the same time offering the offender an incentive and help to change his or her behavior and be rehabilitated.

It is clear that for these purposes to be achieved, the nature and extent of the punishment must be carefully evaluated and decided upon, and ought not go to the extreme of executing the offender except in cases of absolute necessity: in other words, when it would not be possible otherwise to defend society. Today, however, as a result of steady improvements in the organization of the penal system, such cases are very rare, if not practically nonexistent.

In any event, the principle set forth in the new Catechism of the Catholic Church remains valid: "If bloodless means are sufficient to defend human lives against an aggressor and to protect public order and the safety of persons, public authority must limit itself to such means, because they better correspond to the concrete conditions of the common good and are more in conformity to the dignity of the human person." [35]

Despite such official (but not infallible) declarations, despite the growing evidence that capital punishment is the enemy of law enforcement, actually hinders the fight against crime, every public opinion poll in the United States reveals that U.S. Catholics do not differ in their approach to the death penalty from their non-Catholic fellow citizens: a life for a life.

A cry of the heart, the revulsion to capital punishment? Many will surely see this as a heart bleeding for the wrong person, for the murderer instead of the victim, for savage serial inhumans incapable of rehabilitation. There is indeed a danger here. But in our present American moment I find the greater peril in the opposite direction, in a different cry from the vengeful: "Kill the killers!"

In focusing on capital punishment, I fear I have neglected the hundreds of thousands convicted of lesser crimes. Prison chaplains tell us what they have discovered: "that life in prison can be brutal and unfair, that the court system discriminates outrageously, and that we can most often trace the social roots of crime to injustice, poverty and discrimination in the wider society. It is the poor and people of color who find themselves behind bars—and more defenseless than ever." [36]

I have sketched seven categories of men and women who for different reasons can be classed among "the poor" and in various ways cry for life. But these do not cry alone. Listen to the Hispanic communities, in many ways second-class citizens, often ill at ease in traditionally Anglo parishes. Listen to our Native Americans, driven from the land they revere, homeless in their own homes, without work, without hope, wracked by alcoholism. Listen to our Jewish sisters and brothers, fearful as they hear Americans arguing that the Holocaust which consumed six million of their dear ones is a gigantic hoax, never really happened.

How Preach the Cry of the Poor?

My second principal point, the neuralgic issue: How can we possibly preach the cries of the poor? Without any claim to infallibility, let me offer a handful of suggestions that stem primarily from a half-century of experience, more immediately from five years of involvement in my countrywide project Preaching the Just Word.

First, like the Hebrew prophets of old, we who preach must be extraordinarily sensitive to injustice. As Rabbi Abraham Joshua Heschel put it, "To us a single act of injustice—cheating in business, exploitation of the poor—is slight; to the prophets, a disaster. To us injustice is injurious to the welfare of the people; to the prophets it is a deathblow to existence: to us, an episode; to them, a catastrophe, a threat to the world."[37] Some of us surely share that sensitivity; but it is usually those who have experienced firsthand the sorry existence of the poor and the imprisoned, the hungry and the downtrodden. More of us simply deplore injustice; we are against sin; we take up collections for the wasted women and children of Rwanda and Bosnia.

Moreover, there is so much evil and injustice in the world that we grow used to it. We were shocked when TV first brought war into our living rooms; now we can wolf our pizzas and slurp our Schlitz to the roar of rockets and the flow of blood. It's commonplace; we see too much of it; it's part of the human tragedy. It no longer grabs our guts—no more than broken bodies in the Super Bowl.

When that happens, our preaching will not reflect a second significant facet of Hebrew prophecy: we will not "feel fiercely."[38] And we must. When I began to preach five decades ago, the Catholic stress was on the clear and distinct idea. Our seminary education, in philosophy and theology, emphasized objectivity. We were dispassionate searchers for truth, cool critics of error and heresy—beetle-browed, lynx-eyed, hard-nosed, square-jawed. Imagination was for poets. We did not show our emotions, wear them on our black sleeves. Emotion was for women, and women could not be ordained.

But to preach the cries of the poor, the analytic mind is not enough by half. I do not mean that we should rave and rant in the pulpit, play Savonarola, castigate and condemn, flay the fallen flock. I do mean that our people should sense from our words and our faces, from our gestures and our whole posture, that we love the crucified communities with a crucifying passion; that we agonize over the hardness of our hearts, our ability to "eat, drink, and be merry" while a billion humans go to bed hungry; that the heavy-burdened can look to us not so much for answers as for empathy, for compassion; that, within Roman Catholicism, our priestly celibacy has not created crotchety old bachelors but opens us warmly to all who need the touch of our hand; in a word, that we, too, share the dread-full human condition.

A second suggestion: we who preach must understand clearly what we mean by a "preferential option for the poor."[39] The formula did indeed originate within Latin American liberation theology, but it has put its stamp on various levels of the Catholic magisterium. Suggested at the second meeting of the Latin American episcopate at Medellín, Colombia, in 1968, and explicitly adopted during its third meeting in Puebla, Mexico, in 1979, it has been solidly endorsed by John Paul II. It does not glorify poverty, does not canonize the poor. It involves a new way of seeing the reality in which we live, seeing it not from the standpoint of the comfortable and powerful but from the viewpoint of the pressured and powerless—seeing the unemployed, for example, not as lazy idlers but as victims of an economic mechanism from which they do not escape merely by desiring to. It involves a new perspective for reading Scripture, an option "for those whom Jesus himself favored: not the wise, rich, and powerful, but the small and simple, the poor and marginalized." It may lead us "to experience the reality of poor people and even actually to share it, whether temporarily or permanently."[40] It calls us to consider how God wants us to live out the option.

> Not all are called to the same thing. The gifts and vocations are different, the charisms and services distinct, the ministries and functions varied.

What matters is that all, in their own way, are called to translate into action this evangelical priority. For some it will be in working alongside the poor, as one of them and one with them. For others it will be in the effort of influencing fundamental legislative change, on which, in fact, the transformation of society depends. For others it will be in the ability to make the centrality of the option understood by virtue of their lives or their writing, work, and witness. For others it will be in the grace of understanding disease, aging, inability to work, lack of influence, or absence of affirmation as a form of poverty that harmonizes in another key with poor people's own experience.[41]

For me personally, the call quite clearly is to evangelize not only our people in the pews but in even larger measure those who preach, help them especially to understand more profoundly and proclaim more effectively the second great commandment of the law and the gospel: love each sister and brother, especially the less fortunate, as if each were another I, another self. Love them as Jesus loves them; love them as Jesus loves you.

This leads inexorably to a third suggestion: I must preach as if I were standing in the shoes of the crucified. Preaching on children, I must, in a genuine sense, become the "lost children" who sleep on America's streets, the child abused, the child with Down's syndrome, the child wailing for a mother's milk or a father's touch. Preaching on Christmas, I might well ask my people what they see when they look into the Christmas crib. For the Christ child is no longer there; he has grown up, has died a cruel crucifixion, is eternally with his Father. His place has been taken by an African American baby with his mother's drug addiction, by a Hispanic infant with multiple sclerosis, by a poor white child left at a hospital entrance by a desperate mother. Or the crib may be empty because a very little one was forcibly prevented from ever entering it.

Preaching on AIDS, I must become a Canon Barcus pleading with my people, "Help us. Please help us. Be the gospel alive!" Yes, it will help my homiletics if I can cradle an HIV baby in my arms, embrace an infected adult without shrinking. Literally to touch the AIDS-afflicted may well prove the most powerful preparation for preaching as Jesus would preach, were he to walk our infected streets.

Preaching on the elderly, I am uncommonly fortunate. Having turned eighty, I need no longer pretend; I can feel in my flesh what aging is like. Ar-

thritic joints jab, oxygen reaches the heart more painfully, pork and sauer-
kraut trigger a dormant hiatal hernia. I can actually sense in my spirit Rabbi
Heschel's summons to provide the "third age" with a vision, with a dream.

Before I dare to preach (brashly indeed) on women, I must realize that
I have been an intimate part of a culture that took women seriously only
as wives and mothers, all too often regarded them more as sexual objects
than as persons, failed to recognize their singular intelligence, gave little
thought to the extent and depth of feminine spirituality. In consequence,
I must listen to women not only when they offer polite suggestions on
greater equality but as they rage against what they see as injustice within
the churches; I must give ear not only to a loyally Christian feminism but
even to radical feminists who are convinced that in attitude and action on
women the Catholic Church is beyond redemption.

I have been confirmed and encouraged in this approach by a document
approved by the Jesuits' 34th General Congregation in Rome (January to
March 1995) entitled "Jesuits and the Situation of Women in Church and
Civil Society." Acknowledging the contemporary challenge from women,
the delegates declared:

> In response, we Jesuits first ask for the grace of conversion. We have been
> part of a civil and ecclesial tradition that has offended against women.
> And, like many men, we have a tendency to convince ourselves that there
> is no problem. However unwittingly, we have often been complicit in a
> form of clericalism which has reinforced male domination with an osten-
> sibly divine sanction. By making this declaration we wish to react per-
> sonally and collectively, and do what we can to change this regrettable
> situation.[42]

Before I make bold to preach on racial issues, I do well to recognize
that Supreme Court decisions against discrimination do not alone change
hearts, that the Sermon on the Mount has not yet captured all Christians,
that it is not only the Ku Klux Klan and the skinheads who spit on Jews
and turn their backs on blacks, that in point of fact all too many of us de-
spise red folk and black, yellow and brown, all too many still consider the
Jewish people "Christ killers." In fact, rather than say "all too many of us,"
I must look with utter honesty into my own heart, must ask how often,
like the priest and Levite in Luke, I too have "passed by on the other side"
(Lk 10:31, 32).

How share the despair of the refugee, the displaced, yes, the criminal on death row? I see them only on TV, hear their cries, their tears, their silences only via newsprint. A mother cradling her starving infant, a child staring uncomprehending at the tortured flesh of his father, the unforgettable girl-child racing down a Vietnam road ablaze with napalm. The spasms of a blindfolded human as thousands of volts slam into his bound body. Perhaps I do best simply to weep—weep for images of Christ on their own calvaries.

A fourth suggestion: to preach effectively on issues of justice, I should take to heart an expression heard repeatedly across Latin America: "The poor evangelize us." [43] So many of the poor—young and aging, AIDS-afflicted and homeless, women and blacks, Hispanics and Native Americans—have helped the churches discover what a 1979 conference of Latin American bishops called "the evangelizing potential of the poor." [44] How do the poor actualize that potential? Challenging the churches by their overwhelming numbers, by their ever-worsening misery, by their Christlike endurance under domination and persecution, by their underlying gospel goodness, by their simplicity and solidarity, by their openness to God and what God permits, they have in some measure turned the churches around, compelled us to look within ourselves, stimulated profound conversion.

Each year during my twelve years as theologian-in-residence at Georgetown University, I watched ten or so graduates leave for a year with the poor in Nicaragua and Peru, many others for a year or two with the International Jesuit Volunteer Corps in Micronesia, Belize, and Nepal. None of them returned to the States the same; all had lived the hurts of the poor, experienced a conversion that changed them to the depths of their being. I remember talking with a young Georgetown woman who was spending hours in downtown D.C. with drug addicts, battered women, prostitutes. College life had taken on a different look; even the university pub looked different—not bad, just a little sad. I remember Georgetown choir members who sang liturgy at the D.C. jail. They touched what it feels like to live without windows, wear the same old blue jumpsuits, have nothing to do that delights you, languish for months before coming to trial, give birth to your baby behind bars and have the infant torn from you. Words of the Mass that had slipped so facilely from their lips took on meaning: "May the Lord accept this sacrifice at our hands to the praise and glory of God's name, for our good, and for the good of *all God's Church.*" All God's people . . . the prisoners they had come to know.

Sharing the life and work of the poor, their poverty and oppression, their Christian hope under conditions close to desperation, each of these students had experienced what theologian Jon Sobrino has expressed so briefly and so pungently: "When the Church has taken the poor seriously, it is then that it has become truly apostolic. The poor initiate the process of evangelization. When the Church goes out to them in mission, the paradoxical result is that they, the poor, evangelize the Church." [45] Very simply, the poor are not just recipients of apostolic ministry; they are our teachers and educators . . . if we have eyes to see, ears to hear.

An example closer to our daily experience takes us to the elderly who surround us. Henri Nouwen, as so often, has penetrated to the heart of the matter, how the elderly can evangelize us, teach the teacher, preach to the preacher:

> Our first question is not how to go out and help the elderly, but how to allow the elderly to enter into the center of our own lives, how to create the space where they can be heard and listened to from within with careful attention. Quite often our concern to preach, teach, or cure prevents us from perceiving and receiving what those we care for have to offer. . . .
>
> Thus care for the elderly means, first of all, to make ourselves available to the experience of becoming old. Only he who has recognized the relativity of his own life can bring a smile to the face of a man who feels the closeness of death. In that sense, caring is first a way to our own aging self, where we can find the healing powers for all those who share in the human condition.[46]

A final word—a sort of summary. Actually, a story. A remarkable Hasidic rabbi, Levi Yitzhak of Berdichev in Ukraine, used to say that he had discovered the meaning of love from a drunken peasant. The rabbi was visiting the owner of a tavern in the Polish countryside. As he walked in, he saw two peasants at a table. Both were gloriously in their cups. Arms around each other, they were protesting how much each loved the other. Suddenly Ivan said to Peter: "Peter, tell me, what hurts me?" Bleary-eyed, Peter looked at Ivan: "How do I know what hurts you?" Ivan's answer was swift: "If you don't know what hurts me, how can you say you love me?"

I have been preaching for over half a century. As the days pass with ever-increasing swiftness, I resonate more and more easily, if not more and more happily, to the words of the Psalmist: "Our years come to an end like a sigh. The days of our life are seventy years, or perhaps eighty, if we are strong" (Ps 90:9-10). More importantly, each day, each fresh experience, each new pulpit penetrates my consciousness anew, tells me in agonizing accents what each preacher, each Christian, must realize if we are to proclaim the gospel as Jesus did, if we are to transform the earth on which we dance so lightly: "If you don't know what hurts me, how can you say you love me?"

Yes indeed, the Lord hears the cry of the poor. The earthshaking question is . . . Do I?

FOUR

Three Social Issues on an Upsurge

Since completing the expanded version of my Beecher Lectures, I have been urged by an enthusiastic critic of those pages to allot some space to three crucial issues that have mushroomed in recent years but have not been directly addressed in the preceding three chapters. The issues call for consideration here because they have clear implications for biblical justice and can scarcely be neglected by anyone summoned to proclaim the gospel. The issues are (1) assisted suicide, (2) the role of women in the Catholic Church, with special emphasis on priestly ordination, and (3) gays and lesbians. On the other hand, in the context of the Beecher Lectures and my own inadequacies, my treatment of these issues cannot possibly engage them in all their complexities. I must restrict myself to a limited number of critical aspects that suggest the justice components involved, without claiming to solve them definitively. I shall close with a handful of observations on the opportunities and pitfalls that surround the Christian preacher in these areas.

Assisted Suicide

A growing movement in the United States insists that each human person has an inalienable right to decide when he or she has had enough of life, and therefore is justified in terminating it at will, perhaps with the assistance of a dear one or a qualified medical practitioner, especially when life becomes psychologically or physically unendurable.

Legal and Ethical Aspects

The issue rose a significant level in November 1994, when citizens in Oregon voted to legalize physician-assisted suicide. A month later Judge Michael Hogan issued an injunction against the new law with a view to studying its constitutional implications. The legal tangles can be illustrated from two contrasting judicial decisions. In May 1994, Judge Barbara Rothstein of the Federal District Court in Seattle traced a logical line from abortion rights to suicide rights and decreed that the State of Washington's 140-year-old statute banning physician-assisted suicide was unconstitutional.[1] In December 1994, New York Federal Judge Thomas Griesa decreed that there was no constitutional right to suicide. He rejected the use of abortion and termination-of-treatment decisions to argue for a right to assisted suicide; held that the state has legitimate interests in preserving life and protecting the vulnerable; argued that it is not unreasonable for the state to differentiate between refusal of treatment by the terminally ill and a dose of medication that leads to death. As I write, the legal issues seem destined for adjudication by the Supreme Court.

Not a legal expert, I still find Judge Rothstein's decision dismaying.[2] Her precedents are the Supreme Court's abortion decisions. One such decision, *Planned Parenthood v. Casey,* reaffirmed the right to abortion on the grounds that matters "involving the most intimate and personal choices a person may make in a lifetime, choices central to personal dignity and autonomy, are central to the liberty protected by the Fourteenth Amendment." If the right to abortion is central to personal dignity and autonomy, why not suicide for the terminally ill? But why stop there? Why deny assisted suicide to the nonterminally ill who face years and decades of unrelieved pain? Why deny it to those who no longer see any reason for living?

On the sheerly human level, the argument for the "right to die" has a prima facie attractiveness, particularly but not exclusively for men and women who espouse no religious belief, no relationship to a living, loving God. Why prolong intolerable agony? Why continue a living death? Why not "death with dignity"?

The "right to die" argument hides a tacit assumption: that the individual's autonomy is paramount, to the exclusion of other significant considerations. It exemplifies with vivid strokes the rugged individualism that sociologists like Robert Bellah insist has come to dominate U.S. society, where in the last analysis I am responsible to myself alone. A social being with responsibilities to society? Sheer abstractions when your flesh is being eaten away, when your spirit is hopelessly dead.

I am not ice-cold in the face of such situations. I watched my father die of lung cancer, my only brother waste away with intestinal cancer, my mother live six years in a nursing home bereft of reason and memory. Nevertheless, I cannot see them in isolation, removed from the broader picture. There is no moment of our existence when we have only rights, no responsibilities. We are never utterly independent, sovereignly individual, radically autonomous, connected to others only by choice. In this context, I dare not deny two distinct dangers. (1) An unrestricted right to die has potentially disastrous consequences. Very simply, it is uncontrollable. Patient autonomy can move from terminal cancer to mental suffering to terminal boredom. (2) Pressures of different sorts can impact on a patient's freedom to choose. Often there are severe psychological and financial pressures on the elderly and the fragile, dependency burdens that make for a coercive atmosphere, where the freedom of a consent is in fact questionable. The Jesuit theologian Peter Bernardi has supplied a telling example of how easily the right to die can change into the duty to die. It appeared in a letter published in California's *Santa Rosa Press Democrat* from an eighty-four-year-old woman who had been living with her daughter for twenty years. She wrote:

> Everything went fine for many years, but when I started to lose my hearing about three years ago, it irritated my daughter. . . . She began to question me about my financial matters and apparently feels I won't leave much of an estate for her. . . . She became very rude to me. . . . Then suddenly, one evening, my daughter said very cautiously she thought it was O.K. for old people to commit suicide if they cannot take care of themselves.

After recounting the ways in which her daughter had reinforced this message, the woman commented: "So here I sit, day after day, knowing what I am expected to do when I need a little help."[3]

A more recent case in point. Myrna Lebov, age fifty-two, suffered from worsening multiple sclerosis. Her husband, George, confessed to giving her a fatal dose of antidepressants on July 3, 1995. She had told him she wanted to die. But he also admitted to a newsperson that she had become a "burden" to him and that he had told her so. Her sister and her niece, in constant contact with her, were surprised at her suicide. She was highly intelligent, alert to current events, a synagogue faithful, in touch with classmates from Smith, swimming with senior citizens, attending Shakespeare in the Park, eating at a Chinese restaurant, making plans for the future. She did indeed get desperately despondent, but she had agreed to see a therapist and had decided she wanted to go on living. Granted she changed her mind on that July 3 and told her husband she wanted to die. Is it not possible that her depression had once again caught up with her and that she was turning to him *for help?* What might she have decided on July 4?[4]

I am aware of the genuinely desperate cases, but hard cases do not make for good law. The relatively small number of such cases does not justify huge societal changes. Legalization of suicide can only wreak irreparable harm on our societal structure, can only add to the cycle of violence that increasingly threatens our reverence for and commitment to life. In consequence, for all my half-century of agonizing priestly experience with all manner of dying, I am unalterably opposed to the efforts of Dr. Jack Kevorkian to add suicide to the roster of American rights. And in this context I am dismayed by the movement to turn doctors committed to life into dealers of death, whether in a loving home or in an execution chamber.[5]

A Christian Perspective on Suffering and Dying

Since my Beecher Lectures were targeted not to ethicists and justices but to believers and preachers, I believe it is even more appropriate to address myself to suffering as seen through Christian eyes. For the assisted-suicide movement has for background a widespread conviction that suffering is an unmitigated evil to be avoided at all costs. Over and above Elisabeth Kübler Ross's stages of death and dying, "there has been at work in our society a more pervasive and portentous avoidance of the distinctly human experience of suffering. Amid cultural uncertainty about good and evil, suffering has come to be viewed as a secular equivalent of sin, from which we need to be saved."[6] In Christian eyes suffering is a mystery that makes sense only in the context of a God-man's cross. In the context of that cross, suffering is central to a genuinely Christian spirituality.

The prototype of the suffering Christian is the Christ whom St. Paul pictured in his letter to the Christians of Philippi:

> though he was in the form of God
> [preexistent and divine],
> he did not think equality with God
> [the glory he had with the Father]
> a thing to be clutched,
> but emptied himself of it,
> to take on the form of a slave
> and become like humans.
> And having assumed human form,
> he still further humbled himself
> with an obedience that meant death,
> even death on a cross. (Phil 2:6–8)

This is the dying the German theologian Karl Rahner described so eloquently in his last years as he focused ever more intensely on "the cross . . . erected over history."[7] What Paul phrased so baldly and economically, Rahner expanded in a packed and poignant paragraph:

> According to Scripture we may safely say that Jesus in his life was the *believer* . . . and that he was consequently the one who hopes absolutely and in regard to God and men the one who loves absolutely. In the unity of this triplicity of faith, hope, and love, Jesus surrendered himself in his death unconditionally to the absolute mystery that he called his Father, into whose hands he committed his existence, when in the night of his death and God-forsakenness he was deprived of everything that is otherwise regarded as the content of a human existence: life, honour, acceptance in earthly and religious fellowship, and so on. In the concreteness of his death it becomes only too clear that everything fell away from him, even the perceptible security of the closeness of God's love, and in this trackless dark there prevailed silently only the mystery that in itself and in its freedom has no name and to which he nevertheless calmly surrendered himself as to eternal love and not to the hell of futility. . . . In the

last resort what happens in death is the same for all: we are deprived of everything, even of ourselves; we all fall, each of us alone, into the dark abyss where there are no further ways. And this death—which in the first place is simply ours—Jesus died; he who came out of God's glory did not merely descend into our human life, but also fell into the abyss of our death, and his dying began when he began to live and came to an end on the cross when he bowed his head and died.[8]

Immensely important, exciting, comforting: Jesus died our death; Jesus died the way we die; in dying, the Crucified followed us. But far more important, more exciting, more comforting is the other side of the coin: we die Jesus' death; we die the way he died; in dying, we follow the Crucified. It makes all the difference in the world. For Jesus did not simply die; he "died into his resurrection." His resurrection completes his death, makes it effective; his human reality was finally accepted into the life of God. Why? Because Jesus surrendered his human reality "unsupported and unreservedly into the incomprehensibility of God himself."[9]

But Jesus' death-into-resurrection does not change our dying automatically, by the sheer physical fact of his last anguished gasp. Our task is to turn a sheer similarity in dying to a genuine following, transmute sheer punishment for sin into a loving acceptance of God's life, murmur without reservation, "Father, into your hands I entrust my spirit" (Lk 23:46). That is why "death is the supreme and most radical act of faith."[10] Our death-into-resurrection, our death precisely as resurrection, is not something you and I can verify empirically. We die not with an unassailable syllogism; we die with a lively hope. Here, too, we follow Jesus. For all that he was God, this man, too, died not with experience of resurrection; he died with faith in his Father, with hope of life for ever.

Now turn realistically concrete. How, in the practical order of everyday living, are we to follow the Crucified? The way we respond touches the Christian to the problem of suicide, assisted or unassisted.

First, the very word *follow*. It is not simply synonymous with *imitate*. *Imitate* has indeed precious precedent in Paul: "Be imitators of me, as I am of Christ" (1 Cor 11:1). Still, as Rahner saw so clearly,

we are not really expected to copy and reproduce the life of Jesus as such. We live in historical situations different from those in which Jesus himself lived, we have a different and always unique task which is not the same as that which confronted him in his own historically conditioned and restricted existence; he and we together form the one Christ of the one and unique total history of salvation, in which, for all our crucial dependence on him and on his historical existence in life and death, we do not reproduce him, but (as Paul says) complete his historical individual reality.[11]

Let me de-Rahnerize that pregnant paragraph. In the lives of all graced human persons, there are realizations of faith, hope, and love which in his restricted life Jesus did not and could not experience. He was a man, not a woman; he was a teacher, but not a scholar; he did not experience old age or Alzheimer's disease; he never even lived to be a Jesuit!

More accurate, then, than *imitate* is *follow,* be Jesus' disciple. And if we ask where concretely, for any and every Christian, independently of time and circumstance, Christ is to be followed, we must answer with Rahner: by dying with him.[12]

But—my second affirmation—following the Crucified, following Jesus in our dying, is not limited to the close of our earthbound existence, to the terminal cancer, the cardiac arrest. In a theological sense, dying begins when living begins; we share in Jesus' dying by sharing his cross through the whole of our lives. Whatever makes for pain—pain of flesh or of spirit—should be part and parcel of our Christian dying. Diverticula or disappointments, colon cancer or deep depression, schizophrenia or the wrenching of my heart, the insecurities of youth and the trembling of the aging—whatever it is that pricks my pride, assails my lustiness, intimates my mortality, takes the joy from my very bones—in all these brief or enduring "moments of dying in installments" we confront the crucial question, how are we to cope with them? Protest? Become cynical? Despair? Cling more desperately to what we still have? Opt for suicide? Or see in each breakdown an event of grace, a twilight that is God's promise of an eternal Christmas filled with light?[13]

Third, such resignation is not sheer passivity. The committed Christian takes seriously the startling declaration of St. Paul to the Christians of Colossae, "I am now rejoicing in my sufferings for your sake, and in my flesh I am completing what is lacking in Christ's afflictions for the sake of his body, that is, the Church" (Col 1:24). Here, perhaps more than anywhere else, we "complete Jesus' historical individual reality." Here my suffering in discipleship to Christ can radiate as grace to untold, unseen men, women, and children from the District of Columbia to Bosnia and beyond.

A splendid example is the French Carmelite nun St. Thérèse of Lisieux, known in her convent as a comedian, the one who could make the other nuns laugh. Dead at twenty-four, she lives as she promised, "I will spend my heaven doing good upon earth." She is the saint whom AIDS patients invoke, the sister whose message of compassion attracts the marginalized, especially the gay and the lesbian. Her message? It is suffering that makes us resemble Jesus:

> Therese sees suffering as purifying us with a fire that can illumine and sanctify—that actually can create in us deeper capacities for future joy. This painful fire, even as it pierces us, invites us to move from the imprisonment of our misery in order to touch others who are fellow sufferers. The torment burning within us reaches out to warm them in their chilling coldness. The terrible separation imposed by our personal agony breaks down—not by reducing its own intensity but by embracing those whose cries of affliction we may never hear audibly. With Therese, we see the great community of suffering humanity, and offer relief to others through our own endurance of sorrow and heartache. We stifle our cry and ask that what we are bearing be applied to lessening the affliction that someone else is undergoing. Therese used even small distress as coin to give away. When tuberculosis began to consume her strength, Therese offered the prescribed daily walk as currency for another. "I'm walking for a missionary," she said.[14]

For a contemporary example of the significance of suffering within a Christian spirituality, I can do no better than submit the experience of the prolific coauthors John and Denise Carmody. Several years ago John was diagnosed as afflicted with a life-threatening malignancy. Recently the myeloma has gotten the better of the chemotherapy, doubling the amount of cancer. In this context, a letter from John and Denise to their friends voiced in profound accents their Christlike reaction:

> It's a roller-coaster life, as perhaps all lives are. The invitation has been to live fully, gratefully, while practicing the art of dying. You will remember that learning to die is one of Plato's descriptions of philosophy, the love of wisdom. You will also remember that the Johannine Jesus, our current study project, works signs and dies to offer us eternal life. Dying/living.

Learning to die while loving living. Realizing that an incarnate divinity knows this bi-phased rhythm of human existence from within. Trying therefore to become, not callous about pain or death, nor presumptuous, but free of their power to loom up as frightening idols and block out the far greater reality of God. Any of our lives is a small thing. Measured by the calipers of astro-physical evolution, it does not stretch for a micro-inch. And yet each of our lives stands before God, comes directly from God, utterly clear in its specificity, for God, having no limits, is not over-come by the swarm of us creatures but in the divine patience out of time can love each of us just for ourselves. So we wait, letting our aging, sick-ening bodies instruct us as much as our minds, and remembering that we have not been called servants but friends.[15]

In perhaps a single sentence, a Christian spirituality of suffering and dying comes down to a profoundly simple observation of Jesus: only if you lose your "self" *(psyche)* for my sake will you save your "self" (Lk 9:24).[16] Only if suffering transforms me into the Jesus en route to Jerusalem will suffering, daily dying, make experiential sense, let me leap for joy. Each day, "Father, into your hands I entrust my spirit." My spirit . . . all that is my self, the whole of my living/dying self. Into your hands. End to argument, end of the early, self-justifying Job. Now only the dying/rising Christ . . . the dying/rising Christian.

I realize that for some feminist theologians no symbol is more prob-lematic than the cross.[17] It is seen as a "scapegoat syndrome" encouraging women to accept the role of passive victims, especially in the context of contemporary violence against women and children. Elisabeth Schüssler Fiorenza "argues that theologies of the cross glorify suffering even when, as in the case of Asian feminists, identification with the suffering Jesus pro-vides comfort in the harsh reality of women's lives."[18] My own approach to suffering comes closer to that of feminist theologians like Elizabeth John-son, for whom the cross stands in history as a "life-affirming protest against all torture and injustice, and as a pledge that the transforming power of God is with those who suffer to bring about life for others."[19] I shall con-tinue to insist that a genuinely Christian soteriology based on the historical Jesus and the theology of Paul does not "glorify" suffering. It grants that sheer suffering is not a good. But it submits that suffering can be trans-muted into sacrifice through love, that this took place preeminently in Jesus, and that such sacrifice was and continues to be redemptive, liberating. An authentically scriptural soteriology will never cease to echo Paul declaring to the Christians of Galatia, "I have been crucified with Christ; and it is no longer I who live, but it is Christ who lives in me. And the life I now live in the flesh I live by faith in the Son of God, who loved me and gave himself for me" (Gal 2:19-20).

Passivity? Not if you take Jesus at his word: "This is why the Father loves me: because I lay down my life in order to take it up again. No one takes [or: has taken] it from me, but I lay it down of my own accord" (Jn 10:17-18). Similarly, death for a Christian is an "I do." I, this unrepeatable image of God, entrust my spirit. Not by self-destruction; by self-giving. It is Ignatius Loyola's joyous prayer, the prayer repeated in 1983 by Pedro Arrupe, his successor as superior general of the Society of Jesus, when a cerebral thrombosis left him helpless, all but speechless, forced him to relinquish the reins of the Order he had led with such crucified love for eighteen years: "Take, O Lord, and receive all my liberty, my memory, my understanding, my whole will, all I have and all I possess. You gave them to me; to you, Lord, I return it [all]. It is all yours; dispose of it entirely as you will. Give me your love and your grace; this is enough for me."[20]

Role of Women in the Catholic Church

Contemporary conflictual debate on the role of women within Roman Catholicism, with special stress on priestly ordination, calls for some historical perspective. Twenty centuries of pertinent evidence cannot be locked into a few pages, but a swift overview of papal teaching over the past century can set the stage for today's confrontation between feminist cries for justice and Pope John Paul II's "definitive" rejection of women's ordination.[21]

From Leo XIII to Paul VI

There has indeed been growth in papal understanding of woman. In 1891, in the context of exploitation of women and children in the labor market, Leo XIII declared that God has granted equal dignity to woman and man, a dignity that must be respected; that a guiding principle for social development is the right of all people to participate in society. Still, he saw woman's participation in terms of the home, the upbringing of children, for which nature has fitted her.[22] Pius X (1903-14) rarely spoke on woman in society, admired to a large extent the feminist desire for intellectual and social improvement, but was skeptical of women in politics. Benedict XV (1914-22), preoccupied by World War I and its aftermath, could do little but restate Leo's vision of women, stressing the domestic facet of their nature.

Pius XI (1922-39) was to some extent traditional, to some extent progressive. On the one hand, he insisted that a modern error in need of correction was the challenge to "the honorable and trusting obedience which the woman owes to the man. Many [feminists] even go further and assert that such a subjection of one party to the other is unworthy of human dignity, that the rights of husband and wife are equal." Pius saw this as a perilous "debasing" of the "rational and exalted liberty which belongs to the noble office of a Christian woman and wife." This high vocation is hers as a consequence of "the natural disposition and temperament of the female sex."[23] On the other hand, he railed against the abuse of women and children by those who control the means of production, gave unqualified support to the principle of a family wage, and encouraged women to be active in social movements.[24]

Without directly criticizing the emergence of women in public life, Pius XII (1939-58) saw in it a direct consequence of the industrialization of the Western world and suggested undesirable effects when women are compelled to surrender unconditionally to the modern movement. For him, this movement was not the social ideal. Both the law of nature and the Christian perspective called for married women to establish the home, arrange for a husband's well-being, and assure the family of a peaceful life together; the fullness of a married woman's vocation is achieved in childbearing. The God-given dignity of woman can be achieved in any one of three ways: (1) the highest calling: consecrated virginity in religious life; (2) next in preference: marriage and motherhood; (3) the poorest choice: single life in the world, "unmarried despite herself"—a kind of mystery where a woman is encouraged to enter "feminine" occupations such as the classroom, orphanages, and welfare work with released prisoners and "fallen" women. To his credit, Pius XII recognized that the new realities in woman's existence were here to stay, that the Church had to confront these realities in fresh, creative fashion.[25]

In his 1963 encyclical *Pacem in terris (Peace on Earth),* John XXIII saw the participation of women in public and social life as one of the "signs of the times." Today's world, he insisted, cannot tolerate women being treated as inferior to men; they should be encouraged to achieve their full potential for the benefit of all of society.[26]

It was the pontificate of Paul VI (1963–78) that revealed genuinely critical study on the contemporary status of women. His 1967 encyclical *Populorum progressio (The Development of Peoples)* insisted on the right and duty of all persons to develop their qualities and talents to the fullest extent possible, insisted that the struggle against gender injustice must have for purpose the development of humanity as God intended it. Those broad perspectives were spelled out in his 1971 apostolic letter *Octogesima adveniens (A Call to Action).* There he not only reasserted woman's equality with man in God's eyes, but declared that this equality entitled women to participate in all aspects of social, cultural, economic, and political life. The following year his apostolic letter *Ministeria quaedam (On the Question of Ministry)* returned to the laity the roles of lector and acolyte, but refused these offices to women—this on the basis of the Church's constant tradition. In reaction to the pressures of the women's liberation movement in the early 1970s, Paul established the Commission for the Role of Women in the Church and Society. In its report of January 31, 1976, the commission recommended to the Holy See and the bishops that women should have a greater presence within the Curia, especially on issues directly affecting women; that women be given greater access to all nonordained liturgical and pastoral ministries; that in the projected revision of canon law all baptized Catholics be granted participation in jurisdiction; and that women be offered more opportunities for spiritual, doctrinal, and pastoral formation. Catholic universities were urged to employ interdisciplinary study and research for the improvement of the man/woman relationship in society and the Church.

Within two years, in response to requests from bishops' conferences and in reaction to demands for ordination from Catholic women, Paul approved and confirmed a significant 1976 document from the Sacred Congregation for the Doctrine of the Faith, *Inter insigniores (Declaration on Certain Questions regarding the Admission of Women to the Ministerial Priesthood).* The crucial argument of the declaration is that the Church is not empowered to change its teaching on an exclusively male priesthood because this is an immutable truth handed down through the centuries of the Church's tradition. A further argument—*ex convenientia,* to show the theological reasonableness of the primary argument, its "profound fittingness"—contends that only a male can act "in the person of Christ" at the Eucharist, because this ministry calls for a "natural resemblance" between Christ and his minister. "In actions which demand the character of ordination and in which Christ himself, the author of the Covenant, the Bridegroom and Head of the Church, is represented, exercising his ministry of salvation—which is in the highest degree the case of the Eucharist—his role (this is the original sense of the word *persona*) must be taken by a man." [27] This, the congregation insisted, does not detract from woman's dignity and vocation; rather, it makes clear the gender roles appropriate to men and women as revealed by Christ.

John Paul II

Such is the more immediate tradition on woman inherited by John Paul II. In his 1981 encyclical *Laborem exercens (On Human Work)* he objected to women working outside the home apart from genuine economic necessity, proposed a single salary for the male worker sufficient for the family, and argued for just remuneration of mothers in recognition of their contribution to society. Later the same year, his apostolic exhortation on the role of the Christian family, *Familiaris consortio,* had for springboard the signs of the times. He insisted that, as images of God, women have a dignity equal to that of men; that this dignity was revealed in incomparable fashion when God's Son took flesh of Mary; that this dignity and equality were confirmed by Jesus' own words and actions, significantly in his Easter appearance to a woman before the other disciples; that in consequence women should always be seen as persons, not as objects. While recognizing the contemporary movement to see in women more than wives and mothers, he warned against devaluing their maternal and family roles.[28]

For all the importance of previous papal pronouncements, it is with John Paul II that the Church's official stance on the role of women has become a worldwide preoccupation and a source of bitter controversy inside and outside Roman Catholicism. His 1988 apostolic letter *Mulieris dignitatem,* a guide to the Church on woman's dignity and vocation, confirmed the 1976 teaching of the Congregation for the Doctrine of the Faith, *Inter insigniores:* the Church has no authority from Christ to ordain women.[29]

John Paul did agree with a recommendation of the 1987 Synod of Bishops for "a further study of the anthropological and theological bases that are needed in order to solve the problems connected with the meaning and dignity of being a woman and being a man." And to his credit, in *Mulieris dignitatem* he engages personally in that study. He finds in Genesis God's revelation from the beginning that "man and woman are human beings to an equal degree, both are created in God's image."[30]

Where precisely does John Paul discover such equal imaging of God? In the rationality and freedom male and female enjoy, both capable of knowing and loving God. More than that, God has shaped woman and man in a mutual relationship, "called to live in a communion of love and in this way to mirror in the world the communion of love that is in God," the love life of the Trinity. To be created in God's image and likeness means "to exist for others, to become a gift."[31]

Besides revealing what it means to be human, to be man or woman, the Hebrew Scriptures disclose what it means to be divine, to be God. Masculine and feminine attributes in Scripture are not an effort to capture the reality of God clearly, unambiguously; simply an attempt to express feebly the utter incomprehensibility of God, the God who is totally Other, totally different. Jesus' Abba is not fatherly in a human way, but in an "ultracorporeal, superhuman, and completely divine sense."[32]

It is in the Genesis story of sin that John Paul finds God's desire for human equality frustrated. It is not that sin has "destroyed" our likeness to God; still, it has "obscured" our identity, "diminished" the relationship of man and woman, their ability to reflect God each in his or her own way.[33] One effect is declared in Genesis 3:16: "Your desire shall be for your husband, and he shall rule over you." Patriarchy, the structural domination of men over women, reveals vividly humanity's ruptured relationship, "the disturbance and loss of the stability of that fundamental equality which the man and the woman possess in the 'unity of the two.'"[34]

Still, God's never-failing fidelity redeems even this unjust domination. Mary, the New Eve, mother of restored humanity, becomes a model for all women. The Mighty One "has done great things" (Lk 1:49) for Mary: "the discovery of all the richness and personal resources of femininity, all the eternal originality of the 'woman' just as God wanted her to be, a person for her own sake, who discovers herself 'by means of a sincere gift of self.' "[35] In Mary, Eve discovers the true dignity of feminine humanity.

Striking is John Paul's portrait of the relationship between Jesus and women.[36] Against the prevalent discrimination against women, Jesus took their part—not simply because he saw them as defenseless, some as socially outcast, but because he was aware of their dignity, their worth in God's eyes, because he was one with God's original dream of equal personhood. And women responded to him in their distinctive ways, in their sensitivity to him, especially during his passion, in their faith and fidelity proving stronger than all the apostles save John. A prime example is Mary Magdalene, "the first eyewitness of the risen Jesus"—in a remarkable tradition, "apostle to the apostles."[37]

With this and much else on woman's worth as background, what has John Paul to say of woman's capacity for ministerial priesthood? Two paragraphs are especially significant. The first concerns the calling of the Twelve:

> In calling only men as his apostles, Christ acted in a completely free and sovereign manner. In doing so, he exercised the same freedom with which, in all his behavior, he emphasized the dignity and the vocation of women without conforming to the prevailing customs and to the traditions sanctioned by the legislation of the time. Consequently, the assumption that he called men to be apostles in order to conform with the widespread mentality of his times does not at all correspond to Christ's way of acting.

The second operative paragraph has for immediate context the institution of the Eucharist.

> Since Christ in instituting the Eucharist linked it in such an explicit way to the priestly service of the apostles, it is legitimate to conclude that he thereby wished to express the relationship between man and woman, between what is "feminine" and what is "masculine." It is a relationship willed by God both in the mystery of creation and in the mystery of redemption. It is the Eucharist above all that expresses the redemptive act of Christ, the bridegroom, toward the Church, the bride. This is clear and unambiguous when the sacramental ministry of the Eucharist, in which the priest acts *in persona Christi,* is performed by a man. This explanation confirms the teaching of the declaration *Inter insigniores.*[38]

Not surprisingly, the papal statement did not stop controversy, research, and publication. Moreover, the Anglican communion had begun to ordain women; on the other hand, the Orthodox churches made it quite clear that they could not unite with a church that ordains women. It was surely in this context that in May 1994, John Paul II addressed an apostolic letter, *Ordinatio sacerdotalis,* to Catholic bishops on priestly ordination. He made it pellucidly clear that he was writing because in some places the reservation of priestly ordination to men was still regarded as open to debate or a matter of church discipline:

> Wherefore, in order that all doubt may be removed regarding a matter of great importance, a matter which pertains to the Church's divine constitution itself, in virtue of my ministry of confirming the brethren (cf. Lk 22:32) I declare that the Church has no authority whatsoever to confer priestly ordination on women and that this judgment is to be definitively held by all the Church's faithful.[39]

Ordination a Closed Question?

On the official level, the question is closed, is not open to further discussion. In a traditional Catholic understanding of the papal ministry, I see no reason why the Catholic Church, through a general council or in the person of the pope, may not declare an issue closed as far as its own adherents are concerned. The First Council of Nicaea (325) did so when the legendary 318 delegates declared through its *homoousion* that "there was no salvation in the Arian Son, a time-bound creature such as we are, out of the Father by a making as we are, Son only by a grace that holds no grace for us. . . . The Son is all that the Father is, except for the Name of Father."[40] Pope Pius XII did so when he proclaimed solemnly that "the Virgin Mary, upon the completion of her life on earth, was taken up to heaven's glory in body and soul."[41]

Generally it is through such dogmatic definitions, the highest level of authoritative statements, binding on the faithful as matters of faith, intimating God's own revelation, that certain doctrinal issues are considered closed.[42] Not closed to further understanding; only that the basic truth defined is beyond legitimate challenge. Not that the Catholic Church cannot teach authoritatively on a level below dogmatic definition; only that to close off, once and for all, further theological penetration on such a level can imperil the search for God's truth. And it is precisely this that many a theologian finds disturbing in the adverb "definitively" on the ordination of women.

Here is an adverb that claims for itself an authority barely short of the infallible. But if not infallible, what precisely is the binding force of the declaration? The long-time Gregorian University professor Francis Sullivan, progressive indeed but hardly a flaming liberal, expressed his puzzlement a month later. "What level of papal teaching authority does this letter represent?" What sort of intellectual assent is demanded? [43]

Sullivan is convinced that "definitively held" does not demand the response required by a dogma of faith. What then? Cardinal Joseph Ratzinger, prefect of the Congregation for the Doctrine of the Faith, has responded: "It is an act of authentic ordinary magisterium of the Supreme Pontiff, an act, therefore, that is not a defining or solemn *ex cathedra* statement, although the objective of this act is the declaration of a doctrine taught as definitive and, therefore, not reformable." [44] Infallible? No clear evidence. Sullivan concludes that, in describing the teaching as definitive and irreformable, and the assent demanded as definitive and unconditional, "claims are being made for this most recent exercise of what is officially described as 'ordinary papal magisterium' which, to my knowledge, have never before been made about any document of ordinary papal teaching." [45]

Theological Arguments Against Ordination of Women

Two prefatory observations. First, I submit that John Paul II cannot be dismissed out of hand. Not only because he is the spiritual leader of a church that claims divine institution and divine guidance, with a special charism for the successor of Peter. Perhaps even more importantly in the present instance, because he is a first-rate philosopher, a more than average theologian, a man knowledgeable in and respectful of tradition while reasonably open to fresh ideas. His insistence on the equal dignity of women and men, rooted in the image of God; his castigation of woman's domination by man as sinful, as one of the clearest signs of the disordered relationship humanity has with God in consequence of sin; his condemnation of the secular world's disordered objectification of women; his conviction that abuse of women by men is baneful not only for women but for men as well; his affirmation of the responsibilities of both parents for the rearing of children and for family life—these teachings have a depth and a freshness to which today's most modern men and women resonate.

Second, a basic reason why the discussion on the role of women and on women's ordination is so conflictual is not simply the specific arguments advanced by the two sides. The fundamental problem is hermeneutical. As Richard Leonard has observed, "The essential problem lies in how interested parties in the debate appropriate, comprehend and interpret the sources of Christian tradition in relation to women from their own perspectives and in response to the demands of their own world-view." [46] A brief word on this later.

Now for several arguments officially set forth from Rome, specifically in the documents of 1976, 1988, and 1994. (At times one suspects that certain forces in Rome do not regard arguments as essential or integral to an official document's conclusions; the conclusions carry their own authoritative weight. But when arguments are proposed as genuinely probative, a theologian can hardly disregard them. Even if a particular Catholic feels obliged to consider the case closed, he or she is not obligated to pass the arguments over in silence. Arguments are an appeal not to obedience but to intelligence.) As I see them, the most significant arguments in Rome's eyes are (1) Jesus' own call of men alone as his apostles; (2) the constant tradition of the Church, holding the example of Jesus and the actions of the apostles as normative; (3) the thesis that only males can act *in persona Christi.*[47]

CALL OF MALE APOSTLES To begin with, I am personally impressed by John Paul's refusal to accept the thesis that, because of the cultural and religious context, Jesus could do no other than select males as his apostles. He knows that thesis, knows it well. His response? This Jesus afraid or unwilling to act against the times, the culture, the religious tradition, the status quo—this is not the Jesus we know. Weighty arguments for women's ordination still have a place, have to be confronted, but a conforming, complying, complaisant Jesus is not among them. Briefly, in John Paul's own words, "the assumption that [Christ] called men to be apostles in order to conform with the widespread mentality of his times does not at all correspond to Christ's way of acting."

I agree. But for me this agreement raises a question rarely proposed in this context. Granted that, in choosing only men as apostles, Jesus "acted in a completely free and sovereign manner," does it necessarily follow that he intended an exclusively male priesthood *for all time?* Pertinent here is an acute observation expressed by the respected biblical expert Raymond Brown two decades ago, speaking of those who think that the Christian answer to our problem lies in a text like 1 Cor 14:33–34 (women silent in the churches) or back in the creation story of Genesis:

> Here we enter the realm of hermeneutics. Since the Bible contains the word of God *in the words of men,* these texts reflect the sociology of God's people respectively in the first century A.D. and the eleventh century B.C. They cannot be repeated as normative today in a different sociology without first investigating whether the change in social conditions does not require a different expression of God's will for His people.[48]

This observation goes beyond any assertion that Jesus could not do other than conform. It asks: did Jesus, acting "in a completely free and sovereign manner," decide to conform in this instance, in his lifetime, without necessarily binding the Church for all time? Here, I believe, we enter the area of tradition. Perhaps, too, the meaning of tradition. Is Catholic tradition simply "the way we've always done it"? Or is Catholic tradition the best of our past, infused with the insights of the present, with a view to a richer, more catholic future?

TRADITION Over the centuries the example of Christ and the actions of his apostles have been regarded by the Catholic Church as normative and therefore the will of Christ for his community—if not in all particulars, surely in essentials. Granted that (despite some recent but inconclusive historical research in a contrary direction) "the teaching that priestly ordination is to be reserved to men alone has been preserved by the constant and universal tradition of the Church and firmly taught by the magisterium in its most recent documents," what is it about the tradition that compels the papal magisterium to declare that "the Church has no authority whatsoever to confer priestly ordination on women"? [49]

Within most of Roman Catholicism, and invariably on the Church's highest levels, the very constancy of a tradition is impressive and theologically significant. Not that all traditions are of equal value, be they ever so long-lived. Vatican II revealed this vividly when, largely impelled by John Courtney Murray and the American bishops, it reversed the "error has no rights" tradition and declared that "the right to religious freedom has its foundation" not in the Church, not in society or state, not even in objective truth, but "in the very dignity of the human person."[50] Still, a tradition stemming from Christ, on so fundamental a Catholic ministry, over almost two millennia can hardly be overturned save for the most compelling of reasons.

Are there such compelling reasons? Traditional types of argument against the ordination of women have been seriously challenged in recent years by feminist biblical hermeneutics. One significant example is the theological/reconstructionist school of which Elisabeth Schüssler Fiorenza is a particularly powerful representative. She is convinced that "the feminist critique of theology and tradition is best summarized by the statement of Simone Weil: 'History . . . is nothing but a compilation of the depositions made by assassins with respect to their victims and themselves.'"[51]

Four elements specify Schüssler Fiorenza's procedure. (1) The cornerstone is a hermeneutic of *suspicion.* She approaches all biblical texts and theological traditions suspicious that the experience of women is not reflected or recorded therein; for both "Scripture and theology express truth in sexist language and images and participate in the myth of their patriarchal-sexist society and culture." (2) Suspicion leads to a hermeneutic of *remembrance,* an effort to reconstruct the feminist history of the first Christian centuries, to reclaim the memory of New Testament women, known and unknown. (3) To avoid the danger of a liberating vision for women alone, a hermeneutic of *proclamation* looks to the power a fresh interaction between the biblical text and the theological tradition has for the entire Church, an option for the oppressed wherever they be, whatever their situation. (4) A hermeneutic of *actualization and ritualization* goes beyond the appeal to rational faculties and intellectual understanding, provides myths, symbols, and rituals that "encourage particular forms of behavior, . . . embody goals and value judgments," while demythologizing "the myths of the sexist society and patriarchal religion." A significant example is the Mary myth, which for Schüssler Fiorenza "has its roots and development in a male, clerical, and ascetic culture and theology" which "has very little to do with the historical woman Mary of Nazareth."[52]

The long-term objective of this hermeneutic? "As long as women Christians are excluded from breaking the bread and deciding their own spiritual welfare and commitment, *ekklesia,* as the discipleship of equals, is not realized and the power of God is greatly diminished."[53]

The differences between the papal and feminist hermeneutic are clear and startling. Papal hermeneutics, writes Leonard, "works from a strongly defined sense of the archetype that tradition holds and defends it in both the words of the scriptural record and the actions of Christian history." Basing Schüssler Fiorenza's model is "an understanding that, at most, the tradition of the church provides a prototype which we imitate, reinterpret or change."[54] Is there any possibility that the chasm separating the two approaches can be bridged? I am pessimistic.[55]

IN PERSONA CHRISTI Finally, for the purposes of this volume, one of the most important arguments in the Roman arsenal cannot be overlooked: only the male can act *in persona Christi;* only the male has the "natural resemblance" that must exist between Christ and his minister. Two careful scholars give us reason to tread carefully here.

Two decades ago the sacramental theologian Edward Kilmartin argued persuasively that the priest represents *directly* not Christ but the faith of the Church. In consequence, he concluded that

> the old argument against the ordination of women to the priesthood, based on the presupposition that the priest directly represents Christ and so should be male, becomes untenable. Logically the representative role of priest seems to demand both male and female office bearers in the proper cultural context; for the priest represents the one Church, in which distinctions of race, class, and sex have been transcended, where all are measured by the one norm: faith in Christ.[56]

More recently, Dennis Michael Ferrara has contrasted the magisterium's representational view of *in persona Christi* in its rejection of women priests with Thomas Aquinas's ministerial or "self-effacing" view. He concludes that the magisterium unwittingly subverts the proper priority between hierarchical power and priestly service. His final paragraph merits serious consideration:

> The primary sense of the axiom *in persona Christi* for St. Thomas, its chief historical exponent, is instrumental, ministerial, nonrepresentational, and to that extent apophatic. The primary function of the priest is not to

"represent" or "be like" Christ, but to serve as the instrument through whom Christ himself acts, an activity which reaches its defining apogee in the Eucharist, where Christ acts visibly as the principal agent through the ministry of the anamnestic priestly word. There is, however, a secondary and applied meaning of the axiom which does bear an indirectly representational sense, insofar as the priest (or more properly the bishop) leads, presides over, and governs the Church in the name of Christ. *Inter insigniores* knows only the second of these senses, thereby unwittingly placing the meaning of the priesthood as a whole within the horizon of hierarchical power. Reflection on the teaching of St. Thomas allows us to dispel this dangerous ambiguity by coming down squarely on the comprehensive priority of service: the function of hierarchy, in its deepest essence, is not to stand vicariously as lord in the place of Christ, but to call the Church over and over again into the presence of him who alone is Lord until he comes again. And this, to add the pertinent implication, can be done as easily by a woman as by a man.[57]

In a follow-up note Ferrara questioned the magisterium's use of the distinction between (1) the "fundamental reason" why the Church can admit only men to ministerial priesthood (the constant tradition which the Church traces back to the will of Christ) and (2) the theological explanations developed to illustrate the fittingness of the tradition. He believes the magisterium has abandoned the latter argument, the appeal to the subordinate status of women, without offering a theological rationale rooted in a more adequate Christian anthropology. In consequence, the "fundamental reason" becomes unintelligible, because no explanation is given as to why Christ willed to restrict the apostolic ministry to men.[58]

Sara Butler of Mundelein Seminary has responded to both these pieces. Among much else, Butler challenges Ferrara's view that a nonrepresentational, "apophatic" meaning is primary in Thomas's use of the formula *in persona Christi,* and wishes to "show that Thomas regards the priest to be a sign as well as an instrument in the sacrament of the Eucharist, that he presents this mode of signification as unique, and that he understands the sacramental symbolism of persons as inclusive of the natural resemblance of gender."

> *Inter insigniores* neither accepts nor employs Thomas's "subordination-ist" explanation of masculine-feminine symbolism. It draws instead on his general principle that sacramental signs must be perceptible and recog-

nizable, and on his teaching that they represent what they signify by way of natural resemblance. Thomas does not . . . appeal explicitly to the need for symbolic correspondence between the priest and Christ on the level of sex. . . .

Inter insigniores . . . locates the "natural resemblance" to Christ effected by the priest's maleness not at the level of dramatic representation, but at the level of sacramental signification. This outward sign makes his actions vis-à-vis the congregation perceptible as Christ's actions. Maleness links the priest to Christ at the level of the sign, a sign established by the fact of the Incarnation and bound up with the mystery of God's covenant love.[59]

Inasmuch as John Paul II's apostolic letter *Ordinatio sacerdotalis* encountered a fair amount of criticism from theologians, organizations of priests and religious, and associations of the laity, Rome's Congregation for the Doctrine of the Faith thought it necessary to dispel all doubts and reservations on the definitive character of the letter's teaching and on the question whether the teaching itself belongs to the deposit of faith. The form adopted is a response to a *dubium,* that is, a question posed to a Vatican agency about a matter of church teaching or policy. The complete text is as follows:

> Reply to the *dubium* concerning the teaching contained in the apostolic letter *Ordinatio sacerdotalis.*
> *Dubium:* Whether the teaching that the Church has no authority whatsoever to confer priestly ordination on women, which is presented in the apostolic letter *Ordinatio sacerdotalis* to be held definitively, is to be understood as belonging to the deposit of the faith.
> *Responsum:* In the affirmative.
> This teaching requires definitive assent, since, founded on the written word of God and from the beginning constantly preserved and applied in the tradition of the Church, it has been set forth infallibly by the ordinary and universal magisterium of the Church (cf. Second Vatican Council, Dogmatic Constitution on the Church *Lumen gentium,* 25.2). Thus, in the present circumstances, the Roman pontiff, exercising his proper office of confirming the brethren (cf. Lk 22:32), has handed on this same teaching by a formal declaration, explicitly stating what is to be held always, everywhere, and by all as belonging to the deposit of the faith.
> The sovereign pontiff John Paul II, at the audience granted to the undersigned cardinal prefect, approved this reply, adopted in the ordinary session of this congregation, and ordered it to be published.

Rome, from the offices of the Congregation for the Doctrine of the Faith, on the feast of the apostles Sts. Simon and Jude, Oct. 28, 1995.

Cardinal Joseph Ratzinger
Prefect
Tarcisio Bertone
Secretary[60]

Understandably, the congregation's document elicited favorable and un-favorable reactions, largely consistent with positions already held. Here my concern is with canonical interpretations and judicious analyses.

Arguing that the Catholic faithful must assess the authority of the document and understand its message, one of Catholicism's foremost canon lawyers, Jesuit Ladislas Orsy, has essayed a first step toward such a goal.[61] Two questions: (1) By what authority? (2) What is the doctrinal message?

By what authority? Simply, who is the document's author? Established norms for the authority of curial documents distinguish two types of papal approval. Approval *in forma communi* (in an ordinary manner) means that "the pope approves a document for promulgation but does not make its content his own; it remains a communication from the office itself." Approval *in forma speciali* (in a special manner) means "he approves the content of the document and makes it his own; that is, he raises it to a papal enactment." Since the present document carries no unmistakable evidence of "special approval," the rule of law compels the conclusion that "it has the authority of the congregation, no less and no more." And since infallibility cannot be delegated, the authority of the congregation "does not include infallibility."[62]

What is the doctrinal message? On the one hand, the congregation remains within the boundaries of John Paul's apostolic letter: "to be held definitively." On the other hand, the congregation goes beyond the papal text: "[a teaching that] has been set forth infallibly." The two expressions, though close, "are not identical." The weight of the addition? "It conveys the interpretation of the congregation":

A noninfallible organ of the Holy See, on its own authority, does not have the power to modify in any way the doctrinal weight of a papal pronouncement. It has, however, the right to publish its own view, which must be received with the respect due to that office. . . .

All counted, it is a sound conclusion that the doctrinal message of the apostolic letter remains the same as it was on the day of its publication.[63]

On the theological level, how can Catholics be certain that a particular doctrine (here the nonadmissibility of women to ordained priesthood) has been taught with at least moral unanimity by the whole body of Catholic bishops in their "ordinary" functioning (that is, not gathered in council)? As the theologian Francis Sullivan has noted, appeal to a long-standing tradition does not necessarily suffice, for some doctrines with a lengthy tradition have been subsequently reversed: "What has to be clearly established is that the tradition has remained constant, and that even today the universal body of Catholic bishops is teaching the same doctrine as definitively to be held."[64]

Clearly, John Paul II is convinced that such an agreement has existed and exists now, and that the consensus in question has seen and now sees the doctrine as a divinely revealed truth and consequently an article of Catholic faith. I do not deny this. My problem, as a theologian, is the historical data that must undergird such a declaration. It cannot be presumed; it must be established.[65]

Avery Dulles has recently examined, with his customary care, ten of the principal objections raised against magisterial teaching on the ordination of women, finding them substantially inadequate. He recognizes that questions may still be legitimately raised: for example, on the biblical and historical evidence, the iconic argument as currently presented, the precise nature of the assent required, the thinking of the world's bishops. Nevertheless, he concludes that Catholics should give the full assent to an infallible teaching Pope John Paul has requested. Those who disagree should "abstain from strident advocacy" and "pressures for doctrinal change"; and the pastoral leadership should exercise patience and "show understanding for dissenters who exhibit good will and avoid disruptive behavior."[66] In today's theological and magisterial climate, I suspect that neither recommendation will be honored.

Gays and Lesbians

For the Catholic preacher, two broad questions relating to homosexuality are of special significance: (1) How are we to evaluate morally the homosexual orientation and consequent activity? (2) To what extent, if any, can discrimination be practiced without violating ethical and/or biblical justice?

Homosexual Activity and Orientation

On October 1, 1986, Rome's Congregation for the Doctrine of the Faith, in a letter *On the Pastoral Care of Homosexual Persons,* spelled out with fair fullness the Catholic Church's official stand on homosexuality.[67] Whereas previously the Congregation had stressed the natural-law tradition, here it moved Scripture to the center of the argument, claiming "the solid foundation of a constant biblical testimony."[68] It is true that the treatment of various texts from both Testaments has been criticized as unduly facile.[69] In point of fact, however, the Congregation's essential scriptural basis is the theology of creation that it discovers in Genesis, the "spousal significance" of the human body.[70]

Earlier magisterial formulations had stressed the objective moral evil in homosexual acts inasmuch as they "lack an essential and indispensable finality," generally understood as procreation and often criticized as an excessive preoccupation.[71] While *Pastoral Care* does include potential parenthood in the spousal significance of the body, it stresses primarily the relational meaning of sexuality. From the perspective of "the divine plan of the loving and life-giving union of man and woman in the sacrament of marriage," the letter argues that the homosexual relationship "is not a complementary union, able to transmit life; and so it thwarts the call to a life of that form of self-giving which the gospel says is the essence of Christian living."[72]

For many, the most disturbing single statement in *Pastoral Care* is the assertion that the homosexual orientation itself is "an objective disorder."[73] I think it unfair to categorize this phrase as a deliberately disparaging or demeaning remark. Not when the letter affirms the gay and lesbian as often generous, self-giving, with an intrinsic dignity and fundamental liberty. Still, the letter does not set itself to square the disordered condition and the intrinsic dignity.

As for the disordered condition, the letter attempts to dispel what it sees as a dangerous misunderstanding:

> In the discussion which followed the publication of *[Persona humana]*, an overly benign interpretation was given to the homosexual condition itself, some going so far as to call it neutral, or even good. Although the particular inclination of the homosexual person is not a sin, it is a more or less strong tendency toward an intrinsic moral evil; and thus the inclination itself must be seen as an objective disorder.
>
> Therefore special concern and pastoral attention should be directed toward those who have this condition, lest they be led to believe that the living-out of this orientation in homosexual activity is a morally acceptable option. It is not.[74]

Why deny that the orientation is neutral, or even good? Bruce Williams sees the basis for denial in the scholastic axiom *agere sequitur esse,* "action follows upon being." If there were no disorder in *being* gay or lesbian, there would be no reason to condemn *acting* gay or lesbian. This alone is the point of the letter; it disavows any claim to "an exhaustive treatment" of the "complex" homosexual question, confines its scope to "the distinctive context of the Catholic moral perspective." It does not say or imply that the personalities of gays or lesbians are sick, disordered, or depraved. In fact, the letter declares that one's personality is not to be reduced simply to his or her sexual orientation.[75]

Not every Catholic theologian is happy with the appeal to the scholastic axiom "action follows upon being" to justify calling the homosexual's condition objectively disordered. Gerard Coleman, for one, refers to the growing evidence that one's sexual orientation is a given rather than a condition chosen. He raises a crucial question: "In Thomistic language, e.g., if a person is *per accidens* homosexual in orientation, what must we morally conclude about this individual's condition itself? That is, if the orientation has become 'connatural' for this individual, is it authentically understandable to refer to *this person's* orientation as disordered?"[76]

The letter's section on pastoral care has regrettable as well as progressive elements. Regrettable, for many, are the obsessive frequency with which the need to adhere to church teaching is reiterated, a poorly worded allusion to AIDS, a negative approach on civil-rights legislation, and the insinuation that by their excesses homosexuals are largely to blame for violent reactions.[77] Progressive is a forthright denunciation of "violent malice in speech or in action" directed against homosexuals and the insistence that gays and lesbians share in the "intrinsic dignity of each person," a dignity that calls for respect not only "in word [and] in action" but "in law" as well.[78] The Church's pastoral mission is seen as involving not only sacramental ministry and individual counseling but the promotion of fellowship through a call to "the entire Christian community . . . to assist its brothers and sisters" in overcoming their isolation.[79]

Discrimination

Before all else, I believe it important to recognize that documents and statements from individual American bishops and from the National Conference of Catholic Bishops, as well as from the Congregation for the Doctrine of the Faith, have repeatedly urged not only compassion and pastoral concern for the homosexually oriented, but also recognition and protection of their human rights.[80] But to point up the complexity of discrimination, let me focus on a single document.

On July 23, 1992, Rome's Congregation for the Doctrine of the Faith issued *Some Considerations Concerning the Catholic Response to Legislative Proposals on the Non-Discrimination of Homosexual Persons.* In this document the Congregation stated that initiatives to make discrimination on the basis of sexual orientation illegal "may in fact have a negative impact on the family and society." Furthermore, "There are areas in which it is not unjust discrimination to take sexual orientation into account, for example, in the placement of children for adoption or foster care, in employment of teachers or athletic coaches, and in military recruitment." Moreover, it "is sometimes not only licit but obligatory" to limit the rights of homosexuals "for objectively disordered external conduct" and even for "actions of the physically or mentally ill." [81]

The document elicited much criticism, some quite impassioned, from homosexuals and heterosexuals in many countries.[82] In general, Vincent Genovesi argued, "It seems fair to say that this document presents a number of concerns and fears, but offers no proof that extending legislative protection to the civil rights of homosexually oriented individuals or couples necessarily threatens the rights that others currently enjoy and have protection for."[83]

The moral theologian Russell Connors has noted that discrimination is not necessarily inappropriate. We discriminate on admissions to medical school, on selections to an Olympic team, on candidates for liturgical ministry. We discriminate when we frame laws that keep teenagers from drinking alcohol. What is important is fairness. The greatness weakness in the Congregation's document, Connors believes, is its failure to articulate exactly "*why* discrimination on the basis of sexual orientation in the ways suggested is appropriate."[84]

I am increasingly persuaded that decisions about homosexuals and the teaching profession, foster parenthood, coaching positions, housing, and the military are made most fairly and appropriately if made just as they are when dealing with heterosexuals: on a case-by-case basis. Genovesi, I believe, is right on target:

> In and of itself, one's sexual orientation says nothing about one's ability to be a fine parent or guardian. Furthermore, more clarity and justice in this area may result if decisions are made that reflect greater emphasis on the need that children have for loving parents or guardians than on the desire that adults experience for children. As gifts of God, children must never be seen as possessions to which anyone has a right. Rather, it is really children who have a right to the nurturing and support provided by adults who truly love them.[85]

On the positive side, it has been argued that, despite their profound differences, the Catholic hierarchy in the United States can coexist gracefully with the gay/lesbian community, if the bishops are willing to assume the role of a dialogue partner and not simply herald of the truth.[86] The dialogue in question would require a core of agreement, certain basic values that transcend religious or sectarian boundaries and can constitute a common basis for social cooperation.

Does such core agreement exist? A persuasive case can be made. It focuses on the AIDS crisis—the legitimate demand for adequate health-care and basic civil rights. In this context three Catholic values can insert themselves. (1) There is the Catholic conviction that human life is life in community, the divine dream of a single human family. (2) With that conviction runs a principle basic to social justice: social institutions should be ordered in such a fashion that all persons are able to participate in the economic, political, and cultural life of a society. (3) Add to that the Catholic theology and experience of human suffering and dying, linked to a maturing of the gay and lesbian culture to include "respect for a religious element that can serve this necessary function of integrating both pain and pleasure in a healthy and larger worldview." [87]

Preaching on Urgent Issues: The Art of Listening

Much more could be said, and surely with greater insight, on the three issues just discussed. But enough has been said to introduce a similarly urgent set of questions: How ought Christian preachers address these issues? Should they address them at all? Is the pulpit the appropriate locus for sermons on assisted suicide, ordination of women, and homosexuality?

I have said it before: controversial issues need not, on principle, be excluded from the pulpit. Not that a sermon solves complex problems. Even when Rome or Canterbury or Geneva has taken a clear stand, the homiletic problem is not solved. Recall that a sermon is not a catechetical lesson: "Who made the world? God made the world." "May women be ordained? Absolutely not. Why not? Because the pope says no." "Should gays and lesbians teach our children? No. Why not? Because in this instance discrimination is justified." The sermon not only informs and delights; it should be a work of persuasion. Persuasion that stems from a wedding of competence and compassion. It is in this context that I seek to link to these three urgent issues a particularly urgent demand on the Christian preacher. Very simply, I must listen.

Gays and Lesbians

We hear time and again that effective preaching demands that we listen. Listen not only to God speaking through the written Word and in the depths of our hearts, but listen as well to living people as they tell their stories. If we are to preach effectively on homosexuality, we must listen to gays and lesbians. Not only when they speak gently to enlist our compassion, but when they shout out in anger and frustration against our refusal to see through their eyes. Yes, when they insist on joining our parades, when they invade our sanctuaries, when they mock our consecrated Hosts.[88] Not agree; simply listen to what lies beneath the wrath, beneath the sacrilege.

A good example is the interview the editor of the *New Republic* gave to the Jesuit weekly *America*. Andrew Sullivan, Catholic and gay, highly educated, with an evident respect for Catholic tradition, finds it "philosophically incoherent" for the Church to say that the homosexual condition is involuntary and therefore sinless but that its expression is always sinful. He cannot see why a disability fundamental to his integrity as an emotional being should prevent him from leading a full human life of love, why the commitment and fidelity he sees all around him in the gay world is not recognized as good. He agonizes: "Here's someone who looks like a real human being, who is responsible, who can do a job, who doesn't seem to be depraved or dysfunctional or disordered in any more than a usual sense. Do we really think this person merits this particular censure, so much that we could not tolerate being in the same march or organization or pew?" [89]

Sullivan insists that "being gay is not about sex as such. Fundamentally, it's about one's core emotional identity. It's about whom one loves, ultimately, and how that can make one whole as a human being." For him personally, the moral consequences of refusing to love another human being were "disastrous," made him "permanently frustrated and angry and bitter." The Church was asking him to suppress what made him humanly whole and then to lead a blameless life. "We are human beings, and we need love in our lives in order to love others—in order to be good Christians! What the church is asking gay people to do is not to be holy, but actually to be warped." He finds no *positive* approach in the Church to gays and lesbians. Some have been wounded by brusque treatment. In his own home parish, there is "almost no ministry to gay people, almost no mention of the subject. It is shrouded in complete and utter silence." Here is a whole population "desperately seeking spiritual help and values. And the church refuses to come to our aid, refuses to listen to this call." Just a question would encourage: "How can we help you?" [90]

Here is the gay Catholic, the gay child, trying to say "I'm here." But afraid to say it, afraid of being rejected. Do I hear that muted cry? If I do not, how dare I preach about it? If I do hear it, how do I respond? With an unalterable moral principle, or with a cry from my own heart?

If the adult homosexual turns you off, listen to the children. Read the diary entrance from young Bobby Griffith: "Feb. 19, 1982. Why did you do this to me, God? Am I going to hell? That's the gnawing question that's always drilling little holes in the back of my mind. Please don't send me to hell. I'm really not that bad, am I? . . . Life is so cruel and unfair."[91] Bobby killed himself.

The need to listen is particularly urgent where homosexuals are concerned. Many of us preachers, like many Christians in general, are still dreadfully uncomfortable in the company of gays and lesbians. And yet only by listening can we come to see them as persons, as men and women beloved of God, often more gentle, more caring, more compassionate than the straight among us. Only if we listen to them might they be willing to listen to us.

Assisted Suicide

Move now to assisted suicide. How preach on so complex, so delicate an issue? Not by a closely reasoned ethical lecture on the slippery slope; not by an effort to illuminate the fine distinction between killing and letting die; not by an argument for or against cutting off nutrition/hydration. These are important issues indeed, but they are handled more properly and adequately in parish forums or even the weekly bulletin. Remember, the sermon is not so much education as inspiration; ideas of course, but not for their own sake, rather with a view to a response, "What do you want me to do, Lord?" And in my experience our people are led to such a response not so much by indoctrination as by imagination. In a specially effective way, by stories. Stories that illustrate not assisted suicide but assisted suffering. Let me tell one such story.

One evening, ten years ago, I visited an ailing friend in the District of Columbia's George Washington University Hospital. Before I left, she took me down the hall to another room. On one of the beds lay a black lady somewhere near seventy. On her face, all through my visit, was a radiant smile of genuine joy; her strikingly blue eyes seemed to sparkle. She spoke of God as of someone closer to her bedside than I was, spoke of current events as if she were right there in the midst of them.

Since age thirteen, I learned, she had spent much of her life as a live-in servant. She mentioned two little boys, blood brothers, she had helped bring up in Baltimore a half-century ago. She related how she used to scrub the face of the younger boy, Frank, saying the while, "Tad looks good with a dirty face, but you don't." The two lads, she said, grew up to be priests, Jesuit priests; and to her delight I realized, and told her, that I had taught both of them in the seminary at Woodstock in Maryland.

That bedridden black lady, merry in God, in love with people, aglow with life, was totally blind, and both her legs had been amputated. When I left her, I blessed her; but I knew that in reality she had blessed me. And ever since that evening the face of Mary Alice Evans has haunted me. She has ripped love out of romantic outer space, brought it down to a grim earth, made me look at it through her sightless eyes, walk it on her helpless stumps. That lady, never to see again, never to walk again, was more alive than I. She was living out St. Paul's "I am now rejoicing in my sufferings for your sake, and in my flesh I am completing what is lacking in Christ's afflictions for the sake of his body, the Church" (Col 1:24). She lived, she suffered, she joyed . . . for others.

On June 24, 1995, Mary Alice Evans returned to the Lord whose crucifixion she had imaged with incredible joy. The Mass of the Resurrection, before a host of nieces and grandnieces, nephews and grandnephews, cousins and other relatives and friends, was celebrated at St. Gabriel's Church in the District of Columbia by her Frank and Tad.

The Mary Alices surround us, if we have but eyes to see, ears to hear. But not only the Mary Alices, attuned to suffering with Christ, embraced by love. Listen to a woman or man who knows no reason for living. The pain is beyond enduring; nobody cares; relatives are wondering why it is taking so long to die, why death is holding its breath. Before I break the painful silence with my pious platitudes or true-and-tried theology, what have I heard?

Women in the Church

Move now to women in the Church. In Chapter 3 I argued with some passion that we preachers simply must listen not only when women tender polite suggestions for greater equality, but also when they rage against discrimination, and even when radical feminists find no hope for radical change within the Catholic structure. It is not always easy. I recall with some dismay that Milwaukee's Archbishop Rembert Weakland had his wrists slapped by Rome for *listening* to prochoice Catholics on the issue of abortion. Not approving, simply listening. Why was listening regarded as intolerable? Because the case is closed, the disapproval is "definitive." *Roma locuta, causa finita.* Because to listen is to seem to approve, or at least seem open to change. Little awareness that the "case" is not some cold, objective brief, not some impersonal group of faithless protesters. We are dealing with persons, each an image of God, many agonizing over a doctrine they cannot integrate into the actual circumstances of their personal or family existence. The least I can do as a Christian, as a human being, is to listen. For to listen is not, in the first instance, a gesture of approval; it is an act of love.

Moreover, an increasing number of Catholic women are no longer the submissive females of my adolescence, summed up in the old German expression *Küche, Kinder, Kirche*—kitchen, kids, kirk. They are part and parcel of a new culture. Catholics on the whole no longer live within the perspectives of the classical authority-freedom relationship, summarized by John Courtney Murray in one of his magisterial paragraphs:

> Those who hold office make the decisions, doctrinal and pastoral. The faithful in the ranks submit to the decisions and execute the orders. The concept of obedience is likewise simple. To obey is to do the will of the superior; that is the essence of obedience. And the perfection of obedience is to make the will of the superior one's own will. In both instances the motive is the vision of God in the superior, who is the mediator of the divine will and the agent of divine providence in regard of his subjects, in such wise that union with his will means union with the will of God. The further motive, to be adduced when obedience means self-sacrifice, is the vision of Christ, who made himself obedient even unto death.[92]

This classical conception of the freedom-authority relationship had much to recommend it: a vivid awareness of God, of the charism that accompanies authority, of obedience as sharing in the humanness of Christ. But new times have called for a new vision, and Vatican II was keenly sensitive to the new thing. The council recognized two signs of the times as crucial: (1) the growing consciousness among men and women of their dignity as persons, a dignity that demands of them that they "should act on their own judgment, enjoying and making use of a responsible freedom, not driven by coercion but motivated by a sense of duty"; (2) a growing consciousness of community, of each person's responsibility to participate fully in community and to contribute actively to community.[93] In consequence, Murray argued, we must view the authority-freedom issue

> within the context of the community, which is the milieu wherein the dignity of the person is realized. Community is the context both of command and of obedience. Community is also the finality both of command and obedience. Authority is indeed from God, but it is exercised in community over human persons. The freedom of the human person is also from God, and it is to be used in community for the benefit of the others. Moreover, since both authority and freedom stand in the service of the community, they must be related not only vertically but horizontally.[94]

If the traditional vertical relationship of command-obedience must be supplemented by the horizontal relationship of dialogue between authority and the free Christian community, a fortiori does it not make sense for the preacher of justice to listen to the cries for justice that surge up from God's people? Not necessarily agree; simply listen. Why? In order to hear—hear not only an intellectual argument but the cry from a heart. Why hear? So as not to lecture in abstraction but to preach to living, struggling people, to communicate a compassionate Christ.

The imaginative Jesuit William O'Malley once phrased the new situation in delightfully humorous rhetoric about the laity as a whole:

> We can no longer depend on the comforting simplism of "The Church Teaching" and "The Church Taught"; there are too many Ph.D.'s out in the pews now. The magisterium and the People of God are now like Henry Higgins and Eliza Doolittle at the end of "Pygmalion." He had found a tatterdemalion flower girl and turned her into a lady. But once the metamorphosis took place, neither Higgins nor Eliza knew quite what to do about the new relationship. He was no longer the all-knowing teacher, and she no longer the biddable pupil. Not only does the official church have an obligation to listen more to the people, but the people have the intimidating obligation to speak up.[95]

Permit me to close with a personal experience of listening—listening to a woman—that has influenced my own preaching for more than a decade. Back in 1982, I delivered an address at the First National Ecumenical Scriptural-Theological Symposium on Preaching, convened at Emory University in Atlanta by the Word of God Institute in celebration of its tenth anniversary of apostolic service in the renewal of preaching. Central to my address was a long-lived conviction that between study and proclamation there is frequently a missing link. That link is experience: experience of God, experience of God's people, experience of God's wonderful works. That link, I claimed, spells the difference between the workaday, prosaic, uninspired, unexciting, undistinguished homilist and the imaginative preacher with fire in the belly.

I took as an example a real-life homily I had preached on the Second Sunday in Advent at the National Shrine of the Immaculate Conception in Washington, D.C. The topic I chose was "Advent with Mary." [96] My third point challenged not my study but my experience: what does Mary say to us these Advent weeks? She suggests, I said, how we in our time and circumstances are to wait for Christ. Not only for his second coming, "with great power and glory" (Mk 13:26), but for his constant coming each day, in poverty and powerlessness that make his crib look like a castle. Jesus comes to us in the hungry and thirsty, in the stranger and the naked, in the sick and the shackled. Their cry is not only a human cry; God is speaking to us. We are disciples of Jesus, in the image of Mary, only if we listen to that anguished word and act on it, as God gives us to act.

The response to my address from Elisabeth Schüssler Fiorenza was gracious indeed, but stunning and illuminating as well. From ten pages I excerpt only one powerful paragraph.[97] She had already spoken of a distinct danger in a church that restricts proclamation to celibate male clergy: the danger that the male preacher will articulate simply his own particular experience. Acknowledging the experiences that had influenced me (for example, the poets and musicians of my culture), she continued:

> I was surprised that he does not think of taking into account the experiences of pregnant women and their sense of self. I wonder whether the male poets and artists he mentions can give his sermon the detail, sensitivity, and insight that he would need for presenting the pregnant Mary of Nazareth as a paradigm of Christian Advent hope. Instead, listening to the experiences of women with pregnancy, their fears, hopes, troubles, and anxieties, their various experiences in giving birth and their exhilaration in touching the newborn child might have illumined and concretized our understanding of Advent waiting. Yet listening to individual experiences does not suffice. One would also need to study feminist analyses . . . to learn how the experience of motherhood is structurally and societally

mediated and conditioned. One might also listen to single mothers on welfare or to the woman at the checkout counter trying to feed and clothe their children. If the word has to become flesh in the homily, then it must become flesh in the particular experiences of those about whom the homily speaks. And the Mary of Advent is the pregnant Mary, the unwed mother.

In closing, Schüssler Fiorenza declared that "the 'silenced majority' must be heard and allowed into 'speech' again if the richness and fullness of God's presence with us [is to] be articulated and proclaimed today."

Amen.

Notes

Preface

1 From material compiled by John A. Bollier, reference librarian at Yale Divinity School Library, "Bibliography of the Lyman Beecher Lectureship on Preaching," Bibliographical Guide Series, no. 3.

2 George Dennis O'Brien, *God and the New Haven Railway and Why Neither One Is Doing Very Well* (Boston: Beacon, 1986), 121.

1. Preaching the Just Word in Scripture

1 Walter Brueggemann, "The Preacher, the Text, and the People," *Theology Today* 47 (1990): 237–47, at 237.

2 Philip Land, S.J., "Justice," in *The New Dictionary of Theology*, ed. Joseph A. Komonchak, Mary Collins, and Dermot A. Lane (Wilmington, Del.: Michael Glazier, 1987), 548–53, at 548–49; italics in text. Because I am relying exclusively on Scripture for the points I am making in this chapter, it is worth noting that Scripture not only answers our questions but often questions our answers.

3 John R. Donahue, S.J., "Biblical Perspectives on Justice," in *The Faith That Does Justice: Examining the Christian Sources for Social Change*, ed. John C. Haughey, S.J. (Woodstock Studies 2; New York: Paulist, 1977), 68–112, at 69. A Jewish scholar has called biblical justice "substantive justice" because it is concerned

with the full enhancement of human and, above all, social life; and so it suffuses all human relationships and social institutions (Stevan S. Schwarzchild in *Encyclopaedia judaica* 10 [1971]: 476).

4 More recently, Donahue has stated that his "earlier reflections should be supplemented by the reflections of J. P. M. Walsh" in the latter's *The Mighty from Their Thrones* (Philadelphia: Fortress, 1987). "Walsh understands the social dimension of *ṣedeq* by describing it as 'consensus' about what is right. People in all societies have some innate sense of this, even though it differs in concrete situations. Biblical revelation of *ṣedeq* involves the consensus which is to shape God's people. More carefully than I, Walsh relates *ṣedeq* to *mišpāṭ,* the implementation of justice *(ṣedeq)* by action (juridical or otherwise). Finally, he treats *nāqām* (literally, 'vengeance') as the process by which 'consensus' or sense of rightness is restored. The thrust of Walsh's whole work is that the biblical tradition gives a different vision of these seminal concepts than does the modern liberal tradition. In the biblical traditions these terms define a consensus against the misuse of power and disclose a God who is on the side of the marginal" (*What Does the Lord Require? A Bibliographical Essay on the Bible and Social Justice* [Studies in the Spirituality of Jesuits 25/2: March 1993; St. Louis: Seminar on Jesuit Spirituality, 1993], 20-21).

5 Donahue, *What Does the Lord Require?* 12. Here the "image of God" theme is of high significance. In its original context it did "not mean some human quality (intellect or free will) or the possession of 'sanctifying grace.' Two interpretations enjoy some exegetical support today. One view is that, just as ancient Near Eastern kings erected 'images' of themselves in subject territory, so humans are God's representatives, to be given the same honor due God. Claus Westermann argues that the phrase means that humans were created to be God's counterpart, creatures analogous to God with whom God can speak and who will hear God's word. . . . In either of these interpretations, all men and women prior to identification by race, social status, religion, or sex are worthy of respect and reverence" (8).

6 Constitution on the Church in the Modern World, nos. 24, 32.

7 Here I am largely indebted to notes of a lecture given by John R. Donahue during a 1993 retreat/workshop in my project Preaching the Just Word, an effort to move the preaching of social-justice issues more effectively into the Catholic pulpits and congregations of our country.

8 See Norbert Lohfink, *Option for the Poor: The Basic Principle of Liberation Theology in Light of the Bible* (Berkeley: Bible, 1986).

9 Donahue, *What Does the Lord Require?* 14. Note his acute observation that "though it is customary to mark the beginning of the liberation from the birth of Moses (Exod. 2:1-20), the 'revolt of the midwives' (1:15-22) is an important paradigm of resistance to oppression. . . . These women, the daughters of Eve, the mother of all the living, commissioned to bring forth life in the world, reject the murderous command of Pharaoh [to kill all male Hebrew newborns]. They do this in light of a higher law ('fearing God' [1:17, 21]). Therefore 'God dealt well with the midwives, and the people multiplied and became very strong.' On

the narrative level they allow the promise to continue and also prepare for the rescue of Moses from death (2:1-10)" (14-15).

10 The Deuteronomy text allows interest to be charged to the alien.

11 See Isa 1:11-18, 42:1-4; Hos 2:18-20, 6:6; Amos 5:18-25; Mic 6:6-8; Jer 7:5-7.

12 Frederick Buechner, *The Hungering Dark* (New York: Seabury, 1969), 45-46. Note Donahue's observation: "Actually, the biblical notion of sin is primarily social and only gradually becomes individual" (*What Does the Lord Require?* 11).

13 Here I am using the translation and punctuation of Joseph A. Fitzmyer, S.J., *The Gospel according to Luke (I-IX)* (Garden City, N.Y.: Doubleday, 1981), 525, 532-33. Luke, following the Septuagint, does not specify the subject of "anointed" and "sent"; in the Isaian text, however, Yahweh is the subject.

14 These ideas stem from presentations of biblical scholar Sarah Sharkey, O.P., at Preaching the Just Word retreat/workshops.

15 From notes distributed by Professor Osiek at a Preaching the Just Word retreat/workshop. I am indebted to her for these four points as they touch the Prior Testament, the Jesus movement, and the early Christian community; my own study of the pertinent material was triggered by her stimulating address.

16 See the illuminating article by Raymond E. Brown, S.S., "Roles of Women in the Fourth Gospel," *Theological Studies* 36 (1975): 688-99.

17 Ibid., 691-92.

18 The complexity of the "stranger" issue can be found in greater detail in Norbert Brox, "The Stranger in Early Christianity," *Theology Digest* 41, no. 1 (spring 1994): 47-52. A longer version of Brox's thought was published in G. Eifler and O. Saame, eds., *Das Fremde—Aneignung und Ausgrenzung: Eine interdisziplinäre Erörterung* (Vienna, 1991). The digest concludes with Brox's opinion that in Christian antiquity "there were two counter-currents operative in the encounter between Christians and non-Christians. On the one hand, with its doctrinaire exclusivity and almost total claim to possessing the truth, early Christianity delimited and denounced the other in numerous ways. On the other hand, because of the conviction of the divine will of salvation and universality, there was still room for the stranger, for all people, in the ultimate denouement of history" (52).

19 On this text see John R. Donahue, S.J., "The 'Parable' of the Sheep and the Goats: A Challenge to Christian Ethics," *Theological Studies* 47 (1986), 3-31. The usual interpretation—Jesus identifying with his suffering and needy sisters and brothers, a summary of the gospel that serves as a mandate for universal charity—has been challenged. Some scholars argue that Matthew is depicting the punishment of pagans who reject Christian missionaries.

20 Washington, D.C.: United States Catholic Conference, 1974. I make fair use of the chapter on nature because I find a reprise of our situation two decades ago can be instructive for our current situation and efforts.

21 See *New York Times,* Dec. 15, 1973.

22 See Charles A. McCain, manager for development of alternative products, DuPont Corporation, *New York Times,* March 7, 1989; Robert Watson, chief of NASA's atmospheric program, *Washington Post,* Oct. 6, 1989.

23 See Environmental Protection Agency, *New York Times,* April 3, 1989.

24 See Department of Energy, Defense Nuclear Agency, and others, *New York Times,* Dec. 3, 1989.

25 See Bill McKibben, *The End of Nature* (New York: Random House, 1989).

26 David Van Biema, "The Killing Fields," *Time* 144, no. 8 (Aug. 22, 1994): 36-37, at 36.

27 Quoted by Sean McDonagh in a short "Viewpoint" article in the (London) *Tablet* 248, no. 8021 (April 30, 1994): 514.

28 Donahue, *What Does the Lord Require?* 8. See, however, Bruce Vawter, *On Genesis: A New Reading* (Garden City, N.Y.: Doubleday, 1977), 60: " 'Subdue' *(kabas)* is part of the same uncompromising rhetoric within which 'have dominion' falls: literally it implies trampling under one's feet, and it connotes absolute subjugation. . . . Probably no distinction is intended between the two terms even though one is applied to the earth itself and the other to the animals. Man's dominance is declared absolute, subject always to the example of the supreme dominance of God after which it has been imaged." I suspect that the final phrase limits significantly the human application of the harsh expression "absolute subjugation" and brings Vawter quite close to Donahue.

29 Richard J. Clifford, S.J., "The Bible and the Environment," in *Preserving the Creation: Environmental Theology and Ethics,* ed. Kevin W. Irwin and Edmund D. Pellegrino (Washington, D.C.: Georgetown University Press, 1994), 13.

30 Ibid., 19, 24.

31 Jane Blewett, "Social Justice and Creation Spirituality," *The Way* (London), January 1989, 13-25, at 13.

32 Joseph Sittler, *The Anguish of Preaching* (Philadelphia: Fortress, 1966), 12-13.

33 I have used the translation in Gerhard Ebeling, *Luther: An Introduction to His Thought,* trans. R. A. Wilson (Philadelphia: Fortress, 1970), 45-46.

34 For a development of some of these nourishments, see, e.g., Paul-Marie of the Cross, O.C.D., *Spirituality of the Old Testament,* 3 vols. (St. Louis: Herder, 1961-63).

35 Paul VI, *Evangelization in the Modern World,* nos. 27, 29, 34, 36 (tr. *The Pope Speaks* 21, no. 1 [spring 1976]: 16, 17, 19, 20).

36 The exact meaning of *poor* in the Prior Testament varies with different periods and with different types of literature; see, e.g., John L. McKenzie, S.J., "Poor, Poverty," in his *Dictionary of the Bible* (New York: Macmillan, 1965), 681-84. I have simplified a highly complex word.

37 Text in my *When Christ Meets Christ: Homilies on the Just Word* (New York: Paulist, 1993), 27-32.

38 In a message (September 1990) to the World Summit for Children, quoted in an editorial by Anthony J. Schulte, O.F.M., "Make Room in the Inn for the World's Children," *St. Anthony Messenger* 98, no. 7 (December 1990): 26.

39 See *America,* March 24, 1990, 283.

40 The Church in the Modern World, no. 31.

41 Schulte, "Make Room," 26.

2. Preaching the Just Word in Tradition

1 Lawrence S. Cunningham, *The Catholic Heritage* (New York: Crossroad, 1986), 1.

2 From a defensible perspective, Scripture itself can be viewed as part of our tradition. In fact, some have defined tradition as "Scripture within the Church." Here I am obviously distinguishing Scripture from the tradition that is in large measure built upon it.

3 See J. G. Gager, *Kingdom and Community: The Social World of Early Christianity* (Englewood Cliffs, N.J.: Prentice-Hall, 1976), specifically 84-88, 140. A fine summary of this communitarian aspect, with pertinent documentation, is provided by William J. Walsh, S.J., and John P. Langan, S.J., "Patristic Social Consciousness: The Church and the Poor," in *The Faith That Does Justice: Examining the Christian Sources for Social Change,* ed. John C. Haughey (Woodstock Studies 2; New York: Paulist, 1977), 113-51.

4 I am borrowing these themes from Walsh and Langan, "Patristic Social Consciousness," though my own long "life with the Fathers of the Church" has seen them concretized over and over again, and I have fleshed them out here and there. For a good introduction to the social message of the Fathers, as well as a useful selection of texts in English translation, see Peter C. Phan, *Social Thought* (Message of the Fathers of the Church 20; Wilmington, Del.: Michael Glazier, 1984).

5 *Didache* 4.8 (trans. James A. Kleist, S.J., *Ancient Christian Writers* 6, 17). The date of this document has been highly controversial. I tend to favor the conclusion of J. P. Audet that it "does not seem to be much later than the letters of Paul. It may be considered as contemporary with the canonical Gospels. Its most likely place of origin remains the Church of Antioch, in Syria" ("Didache," *New Catholic Encyclopedia* 4 [1967]: 859).

6 Clement of Alexandria, *The Rich Man's Salvation,* 11-17 (*Griechische christliche Schriftsteller* 17, 166-70; trans. and ed. Maurice Wiles and Mark Santer, *Documents in Early Christian Thought* [Cambridge: Cambridge University Press, 1975], 203-6).

7 See *The Shepherd of Hermas: Parables* 1.8-10.

8 Origen, *Homily on the Book of Judges* 2.3.

9 Ambrose, *Duties of the Clergy* 1.132.

10 Ambrose, *Naboth* 1.

11 John Chrysostom, *The Fall of Eutropius* 2.3. For a more detailed, though still succinct, study of private property in the early Church, see Robert M. Grant, *Early Christianity and Society: Seven Studies* (San Francisco: Harper & Row, 1977), 96-123. Note a perceptive observation: "The original eschatological outlook of Christianity made Christians indifferent to wealth, and as the eschatological enthusiasm waned the philosophical ethic that replaced it reinforced a conservative outlook. Christian sermons contain pro forma denunciations of wealth, much more severe condemnations of avarice. This is to say that the rich could remain rich but social mobility was not encouraged. . . . To put it simply,

the Christian attitude toward property tended to be an aristocratic one, and the criticism of avarice was an important aspect of it" (122-23).

12 John Chrysostom, *Homily 12 on 1 Timothy* 4 (*Patrologia graeca* 62, 563-64; trans. *Nicene and Post-Nicene Fathers* 12). Worth noting, in connection with the last sentence from Chrysostom, is Martin Hengel's thesis that "We cannot extract a well-defined 'Christian doctrine of property' either from the New Testament or from the history of the early church. Right down to most recent times, views which have claimed to possess this character owe more to natural law than to Christianity" (*Property and Riches in the Early Church: Aspects of a Social History of Early Christianity* [Philadelphia: Fortress, 1974], 12).

13 John Chrysostom, *Homily 20 on 1 Corinthians* 3 (*Patrologia graeca* 61, 540).

14 John Chrysostom, *Homily 50 on Matthew* 4. See further details in my chapter "The Body of Christ: Patristic Insights," in *The Church as the Body of Christ*, ed. Robert S. Pelton (Notre Dame, Ind.: University of Notre Dame Press, 1963), 69-101, at 95-98.

15 For details see my "The Body of Christ," 98-101.

16 Augustine, *Treatises on the First Letter of John* 10.7 (*Patrologia latina* 35, 2059). The final sentence in the Latin is ambiguous, dependent for its precise meaning on where one pauses or punctuates: "Ergo tota dilectio nostra fraterna est erga christianos, erga omnia membra eius."

17 Ibid., 10.8 (*Patrologia latina* 35, 2060).

18 See Clement's homily on Mk 10:17-31, *The Rich Man's Salvation*. As shown above, Clement argues that it is not necessary to rid oneself of all one owns to be saved. Were this so, no one could support the poor. What the Christian must relinquish is not riches but the passion, the attachment. It is sin, not wealth, that excludes from the kingdom.

19 Hans von Campenhausen, *The Fathers of the Greek Church* (New York: Pantheon, 1959), 10.

20 I borrow much here from the summary article by Edward Duff, S.J., "Social Gospel," *New Catholic Encyclopedia* 13 (1967): 315-16, and from the longer treatment by T. Howland Sanks, S.J., "Liberation Theology and the Social Gospel," *Theological Studies* 41 (1980): 668-82.

21 So the leading historian of the movement, Charles Howard Hopkins, *The Rise of the Social Gospel in American Protestantism 1865-1915* (New Haven: Yale University Press, 1940).

22 Ibid., 79-80.

23 Sanks, "Liberation Theology," 674.

24 Walter Rauschenbusch, *A Theology for the Social Gospel* (New York: Abingdon, 1917), 1. It is this book that "finally gave the Social Gospel its own theology and remains the epitome of the movement's thinking" (Sanks, "Liberation Theology," 675).

25 Duff, "Social Gospel," 316.

26 See John C. Bennett, "The Social Gospel Today," in *The Social Gospel: Religion and Reform in Changing America*, ed. Ronald C. White Jr. and C. Howard Hopkins (Philadelphia: Temple University Press, 1976), 285-88.

27 Ibid.

28 See Robert T. Handy, ed., *The Social Gospel in America* (New York: Oxford University Press, 1966), 259; White and Hopkins, *Social Gospel,* 273-82.

29 See White and Hopkins, *Social Gospel,* passim.

30 See Sanks, "Liberation Theology and the Social Gospel."

31 See ibid., 679-80.

32 See ibid., 680-81.

33 The metaphor "building blocks" seems more appropriate than the "blueprints" popular in the forties, for the encyclicals are hardly precise, detailed directions for construction; see John A. Armstrong, "American Culture and Catholic Value: An Historical Perspective," in *Rights, Authority and Community* (CCICA Annual 1944, vol. 13 [Philadelphia: Catholic Commission on Intellectual and Cultural Affairs, 1994], 88-106, at 98-99). For a useful commentary on official documents, see Fred Kammer, S.J., *Doing Faithjustice: An Introduction to Catholic Social Thought* (New York: Paulist, 1991), 77-120. In fact, the whole book is a splendid resource for theoretical knowledge and practical activism by a Jesuit who currently presides over Catholic Charities, the largest and most effective "doing faithjustice" operation in the United States. I recommend highly three other source-material productions. Donal Dorr's *Option for the Poor: A Hundred Years of Vatican Social Teaching* (Maryknoll, N.Y.: Orbis, 1983) is an in-depth examination of papal and conciliar documents in the context of the Church's commitment to the poor and oppressed. *Catholic Social Teaching: Our Best Kept Secret,* by Peter J. Henriot, S.J., Edward P. DeBerri, S.J., and Michael J. Schultheis, S.J., rev. ed. (Maryknoll, N.Y.: Orbis, 1988), provides historical background to the major Catholic social-teaching documents, notes the major areas of concern, and summarizes the various sections of each document. Michael J. Schuck, *That They Be One: The Social Teachings of the Papal Encyclicals 1740-1989* (Washington, D.C.: Georgetown University Press, 1991), calls it arbitrary to date Catholic social teaching from 1891. Popes, Schuck points out, have been writing encyclicals on social questions since 1740; and so he surveys every encyclical ever written so as to piece together a coherent social stance. Jesuit sociologist John A. Coleman has called this work "indispensable" (see review in *Commonweal* 119, no. 2 [Jan. 31, 1992]: 37-38).

34 Dorr, *Option for the Poor,* 12.

35 Leo XIII, *Rerum novarum* 36 (trans. *Proclaiming Justice and Peace: Papal Documents from Rerum novarum through Centesimus annus,* ed. Michael Walsh and Brian Davies, rev. ed. [Mystic, Conn.: Twenty-third Publications, 1991], 29-30, with slight changes in spelling and punctuation). Walsh's introduction (1-14) has the advantage of putting each document in context (historical, ecclesiastical, political, social, and/or economic).

36 Walsh, Introduction, ibid., 3.

37 Pius XI, *Quadragesimo anno* 79 (trans. *Proclaiming Justice and Peace,* 62).

38 E.g., in his radio address of June 1, 1941, commemorating the fiftieth anniversary of *Rerum novarum.*

39 John XXIII, *Mater et magistra* 54-55 (trans. *Proclaiming Justice and Peace,* 92).

See the useful article by Donald R. Campion, S.J., "*Mater et magistra* and Its Commentators," *Theological Studies* 24 (1963): 1-52, which summarizes "the principal viewpoints expressed" on the encyclical (193 reactions are listed at the end). The "Catholic complaints" (37-38) are intriguing.

40 See my address to a labor-management forum, Reconstructing the Social Order and the World of Work, organized by the School of Business Administration of Temple University, Philadelphia, published under the title "Reconstructing the Social Order: Truth, Justice, Love—and Freedom," *Review of Social Economy* 30 (1972): 200-206.

41 Vatican II, Declaration on Religious Freedom, no. 2.

42 Vatican II, Pastoral Constitution on the Church in the Modern World, no. 93.

43 Paul VI, *Evangelii nuntiandi,* nos. 29 and 36 (trans. *The Pope Speaks* 21, no. 1 [spring 1976], 17 and 20).

44 Paul VI, *Octogesima adveniens,* no. 4. I am using the official English translation of this passage as reproduced by Mary Elsbernd, O.S.F., "What Ever Happened to *Octogesima adveniens?*" *Theological Studies* 56 (1995): 39-60, at 42. I have presumed to add "and women" to "all men," to capture more discreetly the full meaning of *homines* in our day.

45 Elsbernd, "What Ever Happened," 43.

46 1971 Synod of Bishops, Introduction, *Justice in the World* (Vatican City: Vatican Press, 1971), 5. One may argue whether "constitutive" in the document means "integral" or "essential." The 1976 document of the International Theological Commission, "Human Development and Christian Salvation" (trans. Walter J. Burghardt, S.J., *Origins* 7, no. 20 [Nov. 3, 1977]: 311), states that "it seems more accurate to interpret [*ratio constitutiva*] as meaning an integral part, not an essential part" [IV]—a discussable affirmation, though John Paul II appears to have interpreted it in this way in an address on Feb. 27, 1982, to the provincials of the Society of Jesus (*Osservatore romano,* Feb. 28, 1982, 3). What is beyond argument is that the synod saw the search for justice as inseparable from the proclamation of the gospel. The term began to receive critical examination during the 1974 Synod of Bishops, with "constitutive" as "integral" or "essential" fiercely debated. See the important article by Charles M. Murphy, "Action for Justice as Constitutive of the Gospel: What Did the 1971 Synod Mean?" *Theological Studies* 44 (1983): 298-311. Murphy, at the time rector of the North American College in Rome, concluded that "the heart of the ambiguity about the meaning of constitutive . . . seems to reside in differing conceptions of what kind of justice is being referred to. If justice is conceived exclusively on the plane of the natural, human virtue of justice as explained in classical philosophical treatises, then such justice can only be conceived as an integral but nonessential part of the preaching of the gospel. But if justice is conceived in the biblical sense of God's liberating action which demands a necessary human response—a concept of justice which is far closer to agape than to justice in the classical philosophical sense—then justice must be defined as of the essence of the gospel itself. The latter sense seems to reflect better the mentality of more recent Christian

social doctrine" (308). The paragraph strikes me as a splendid clarifying insight.

47 1974 Synod of Bishops, "Human Rights and Reconciliation," *Origins* 4 (1974): 318.

48 See *Justice in the World,* no. 35.

49 Kammer, *Doing Faithjustice,* 98.

50 John Paul II, *Sollicitudo rei socialis,* no. 21 (trans. *John Paul II, On Social Concern* [Washington, D.C.: United States Catholic Conference, n.d.], 35).

51 John Paul II, *Centesimus annus,* no. 34.

52 *Sollicitudo rei socialis,* no. 35 (trans. USCC 68).

53 Elsbernd, "What Ever Happened," 59-60.

54 See ibid., 60.

55 1974 Synod of Bishops, "Human Rights and Reconciliation," *Origins* 4 (1974): 318.

56 So the historian of medieval Christianity Robert W. Shaffern, "Christianity and the Rise of the Nuclear Family," *America* 170, no. 16 (May 7, 1994): 13-15, at 15.

57 Edward B. Arroyo, S.J., "Solidarity: A Moral Imperative for an Interdependent World," *Blueprint for Social Justice* 42, no. 1 (September 1988): 1-7, at 5.

58 John Paul II, *Sollicitudo rei socialis* 38 (trans. USCC 74).

59 Welcome exceptions are Vatican II's Pastoral Constitution on the Church in the Modern World and John Paul II's address prepared for World Peace Day 1990, "Peace with God the Creator, Peace with All Creation," published in *Origins* 19 (1989): 465-68. Still, the Columban missionary Sean McDonagh takes the pope to task because the encyclical *Veritatis splendor,* on the foundations of morality, did not devote a single sentence to "the morality of disfiguring the image of God in creation" ("Care for the Earth Is a Moral Duty," *Month* 248, no. 8021 [April 30, 1994]: 514).

60 See Joseph Sittler, "Ecological Commitment as Theological Responsibility," *Idoc,* Sept. 12, 1970, 75-85; also his remarks in *Vatican II: An Interfaith Appraisal,* ed. John H. Miller, C.S.C. (Notre Dame, Ind.: University of Notre Dame Press, 1966), 426-27.

61 Rosemary Ruether, *New Woman, New Earth: Sexist Ideologies and Human Liberation* (New York: Seabury, 1975), 204. See her more recent *Gaia and God: An Ecofeminist Theology of Earth Healing* (San Francisco: HarperCollins, 1992).

62 Sally McFague, *Models of God: Theology for an Ecological, Nuclear Age* (Philadelphia: Fortress, 1987).

63 See, e.g., Thomas Berry, *The Dream of the Earth* (San Francisco: Sierra Club, 1988).

64 Anne Lonergan and Caroline Richards, eds., *Thomas Berry and the New Cosmology* (Mystic, Conn.: Twenty-third Publications, 1990), 107, 108.

65 Gabriel Daly, O.S.A., "Foundations in Systematics for Ecological Theology," in *Preserving the Creation: Environmental Theology and Ethics,* ed. Kevin W. Irwin and Edmund D. Pellegrino (Washington, D.C.: Georgetown University Press, 1994), 33-59, at 33, 42. I have made extensive use of this essay here, but one should also consult his earlier *Creation and Redemption* (Wilmington, Del.:

Michael Glazier, 1988). It seems clear that Eastern Orthodox theologians have accused Western Christian theology of unjustifiably and harmfully separating creation from redemption.

66 Ibid., 38.

67 Ibid., 40-41.

68 John F. Haught, *The Promise of Nature: Ecology and Cosmic Purpose* (New York: Paulist, 1993). Quotations from, respectively, 38, 65, 87, 139, and 137.

69 Pastoral Constitution on the Church in the Modern World, no. 57. The same document has a section (39) on a new earth God is preparing "where justice will have its home," when "all that creation which God fashioned for humanity's sake will be delivered from vanity's bondage."

70 English text, "Peace with All Creation," in *Origins* 19, nos. 28 (Dec. 14, 1989): 465-68. Quotation from no. 8; emphasis mine.

71 Ibid., no. 15 (*Origins*, 468).

72 William J. Byron, "The Future of Catholic Social Thought," *New Theology Review* 6, no. 4 (November 1993): 41-53.

73 Ibid., 47-48.

74 Such suggestions simply highlight the type of thinking whereby "bishops' conferences and their advisers, along with Catholic intellectuals and social-service providers around the world, could, after contact with people on all the margins, agree upon a comprehensive set of categories that cover social life, and come up with appropriate social questions to which a thinking and teaching Church would have something important to say in each of these categories" (ibid., 52-53).

75 Pastoral Constitution on the Church in the Modern World, no. 35.

76 John Paul II, *Sollicitudo rei socialis*, no. 28 (trans. USCC 48-50).

77 Another possible translation of verse 2: "Day after day they [the heavens] pour forth His word; night after night it [the firmament] declares His knowledge" (so John S. Kselman, S.S., and Michael L. Barré, S.S., "Psalms," *The New Jerome Biblical Commentary*, ed. Raymond E. Brown, S.S., Joseph A. Fitzmyer, S.J., and Roland E. Murphy, O.Carm. [Englewood Cliffs, N.J.: Prentice Hall, 1990], 34:37, p. 529).

78 See, e.g., George Higgins, "The Problems in Preaching: Politics/What Place in Church?" *Origins* 2, no. 13 (Sept. 21, 1972): 207, 212-16, still valuable for its wedding of the theoretical and the practical, based on the respected author's long and varied experience in social areas.

79 Pastoral Constitution on the Church in the Modern World, no. 43. In this connection I commend to preachers a splendid cautionary article by George G. Higgins, "The Social Mission of the Church after Vatican II," *America* 155, no. 2 (July 19-26, 1986): 25-29. Msgr. Higgins agrees with Karl Rahner that "clerical zeal for social reform . . . ought to be coupled with a realistic recognition of the fact that the clergy really do not have the answers to all of the complicated problems confronting the modern world" (27). He suggests that "even the most radical kind of social reform . . . should be compatible with a decent respect for technical expertise and the legitimate autonomy of the temporal order and also with a reasonable measure of what used to be known as liberal tolerance" (27).

And though he fully agrees that "liberation is absolutely essential to evangelization," he notes that "the church cannot find a future simply in secular concerns, however pressing and urgent these may be, for *the church is meant to be a community of the transcendent*" (28; emphasis mine).

80 Quoted by Joel Porte, "I Am Not the Man You Take Me For," *Harvard Magazine* 81, no. 5 (May-June 1979): 50-51.

3. Preaching the Cry of the Poor

1 The widow of Lk 18:1-8 is not utterly powerless, of course: "She persistently makes her complaint in a courtroom until justice prevails. Although contemporary readers may not see any incongruity, Jesus' first audience would have been startled at the thought of a woman arguing her own case in court. Such a duty would ordinarily have been assumed by her nearest male relative, who would have taken responsibility for her at the death of her husband. This may have led the audience to assume that her complaint was against the very man who should have been her protector!" (Barbara Reid, O.P., "The Ethics of Luke," *The Bible Today* 31 [1993]: 283-87, at 284).

2 See Mary Rose McGeady, *God's Lost Children: Letters from Covenant House* (New York: Covenant House, 1991), 31.

3 Ibid.

4 I have taken the U.N. data from a summary article in the *Kansas City Star* for Sept. 26, 1993, which reproduces an article by Gayle Reaves in the *Dallas Morning News*. For up-to-date detailed information, see *The State of America's Children Yearbook* (Washington, D.C.: Children's Defense Fund, 1995). Important data may also be found in the Children's Defense Fund's *Unshared Sacrifice: The House of Representatives' Shameful Assault on America's Children,* rev. ed. (Washington, D.C.: Children's Defense Fund, 1995).

5 See the editorial "Children Too Ready To Die Young," *Washington Post,* Nov. 3, 1993.

6 Robert F. Drinan, "A New Worldwide Commitment to the Rights of Children," *America* 169, no. 11 (Oct. 16, 1993): 22-23, at 23.

7 In Edelman's Introduction to Arloc Sherman, *Wasting America's Future: The Children's Defense Fund Report on the Costs of Child Poverty* (Boston: Beacon, 1994), xv, xviii-xix; emphasis in text.

8 For details see Sherman, *Wasting America's Future,* 9-57.

9 It would appear, however, that the Clinton Administration "has all but pledged it would recommend that the U.S. Senate ratify the convention" (Drinan, "A New Worldwide Commitment," 23).

10 Michael Kinsley, "Class Warfare? Tell Me about It," *Time* 145, no. 5 (Feb. 6, 1995): 80.

11 From excerpts in *Catholic Health World* 4, no. 13 (July 1, 1988): 1, 12, with corrections from a text graciously supplied by the editor of that journal.

12 See the informative, question-raising article by William C. Spohn, S.J., "The Moral Dimensions of AIDS," *Theological Studies* 49 (1988): 89-109.

13 Cardinal Joseph Bernardin, "The Church's Response to the AIDS Crisis," *Origins* 16, no. 22 (Nov. 13, 1986): 383-85, at 384. See also *AIDS, Ethics, and Religion: Embracing a World of Suffering,* ed. Kenneth R. Overberg, S.J. (Maryknoll, N.Y.: Orbis, 1994), a broad introduction to the reality of AIDS, challenging myths and misconceptions.

14 See Francis V. Tiso, ed., *Aging: Spiritual Perspectives* (Lake Worth, Fla.: Sunday Publications, 1982).

15 Asher Finkel, "Aging: The Jewish Perspective," in Tiso, *Aging,* 130.

16 Quoted ibid., 133.

17 Maria Riley, O.P., and Nancy Sylvester, I.H.M., *Trouble and Beauty: Women Encounter Catholic Social Teaching* (Washington, D.C.: Center of Concern et al., 1991), 6.

18 See ibid., 13.

19 See Joan Chittister, O.S.B., *Job's Daughters: Women and Power* (New York: Paulist, 1990).

20 Riley and Sylvester, *Trouble and Beauty,* 13.

21 See ibid., 14.

22 From Norma Hardy, *Ecumenical Decade 1988-1998: Churches in Solidarity with Women: Prayers and Poems, Songs and Stories* (Geneva: World Council of Churches, 1988), 68.

23 I am borrowing from the text in *Sister Thea Bowman, Shooting Star: Selected Writings and Speeches,* ed. Celestine Cepress, FSPA (Winona, Minn.: Saint Mary's Press, 1993), 31, itself taken from *Origins* 6 (1989): 114-18.

24 Numbers, as of Dec. 31, 1993, are taken from *World Refugee Survey 1994* (Washington, D.C.: U.S. Committee for Refugees, 1994), 40-41.

25 Numbers provided me by the U.S. Committee on Refugees, as of April 1994. The "Selected List of Significant Populations of Internally Displaced Persons" in *World Refugee Survey 1994,* 42, presents only reported estimates, and no total, because "information on internal displacement is fragmentary."

26 For specific figures see Kevin Cahill, M.D., ed., *Clearing the Fields* (New York: Basic Books, 1994); a summary of some of the pertinent data has been supplied by James S. Torrens, "Clearing the Fields," *America* 172, no. 3 (Feb. 4, 1995): 20. See also Robin Lubbock, "World's Land Mines Kill 25 People a Day," *National Catholic Reporter* 31, no. 14 (Feb. 3, 1995): 14.

27 Lubbock, "World's Land Mines, 14."

28 *Arms Trade News,* February 1996, 1. The International Campaign to Ban Landmines challenges the focus of the review conference, in the conviction that there can be no technological solution to the land mines crisis; a total ban on antipersonnel mines is imperative.

29 For useful, up-to-date information, as well as ethical evaluations, see Jef van Gerwen, S.J., *Antipersonnel Land Mines: An Ethical Reflection* (Discovery: Jesuit International Ministries 6, September 1995; St. Louis: Institute of Jesuit Sources, 1995). The booklet contains several important pages (32-36) by Senator Leahy, who realizes that the moratorium he introduced is only a beginning but is convinced that it "could be the spark that leads to international cooperation to stop

this senseless slaughter. What we do is watched around the globe" (35). See also K. C. Swanson, "Pentagon's Fighting a Ban on Mines," *National Journal,* Feb. 17, 1966, 370-71.

30 Robert M. Morgenthau, "What Prosecutors Won't Tell You," *New York Times,* Feb. 7, 1995. The arguments that follow are largely indebted to the factual information he provides.

31 Ibid.

32 On manifest unfairness in the judicial treatment of the wealthy and the indigent, see Nick Dispoldo, "Capital Punishment and the Poor," *America* 172, no. 4 (Feb. 11, 1995): 18-19. For the argument that the high cost of the death penalty sacrifices more effective services to the community, see the moving article by Michael Ross, "A Voice from Death Row," *America* 172, no. 4 (Feb. 11, 1995): 6-7. Ross's own death sentence has since been voided by the Supreme Court of Connecticut for errors in the sentencing process. As of February 1996 no new sentence had been pronounced.

33 Robert F. Drinan, S.J., "Catholics and the Death Penalty," *America* 170, no. 21 (June 18, 1994): 13-15, at 14.

34 See ibid. for details. See also the careful analysis by John Langan, S.J., "Capital Punishment," *Theological Studies* 54 (1993): 111-24. Langan discusses the 1992 document of the Catholic Bishops' Conference of the Philippines opposing President Fidel Ramos' reinstatement of capital punishment as part of his anticrime program; law professor Mark Tushnet's conviction that "abolition of capital punishment . . . would amount to a . . . denial of the actual condition of society in the United States" (116); special problems for the medical profession, e.g., psychiatrists restoring the mentally disturbed to sufficient competence for execution; the fact that capital punishment "resolves only a minute fraction of the crime problem that so troubles our society" (122). He finds "both reasonable and right" the ecumenical statement by the Christian religious leaders of Arizona, "The death penalty cannot be justified as a legitimate tool of society's justice system" (124). In an article at once well-reasoned and compassionate, "The Death Penalty and the Catholic Conscience," *St. Anthony Messenger* 102, no. 8 (January 1995), theologian Kenneth R. Overberg, S.J., offers a persuasive presentation of the more powerful arguments for abolition of capital punishment.

35 John Paul II, encyclical letter *Evangelium vitae (The Gospel of Life)* 56 (trans. *Origins* 24, no. 42 [April 6, 1995]: 709). The phrase within quotation marks is taken from the *Catechism of the Catholic Church,* no. 2267. According to Cardinal Joseph Ratzinger, the discussion of the death penalty in the *Catechism* will be revised to reflect the stronger reservations expressed by the pope (*Origins,* ibid., 689).

36 Dean Brackley, S.J., "A Theology for Criminal Justice Advocates," in *Who Is the Prisoner? A Better Christian Response,* ed. George Anderson, S.J., et al., 2d ed. (New Orleans: Loyola University Institute of Human Relations, 1992), 197-212, at 197. The whole issue of twenty-nine articles, most by hands-on ministers, is impressively informative.

37 Abraham J. Heschel, *The Prophets* (New York: Harper & Row, 1962), 4.

38 Ibid.
39 In what follows I am much indebted to Marcello de Carvalho Azevedo, "Option for the Poor: God's Pedagogy," *Review for Religious,* November–December 1993, 886–92.
40 Ibid. 888, 889.
41 Ibid., 891–92. An effort to achieve greater clarity in specifying the ethical requirements of the preferential option is discoverable in Stephen J. Pope, "The 'Preferential Option for the Poor': An Ethic for 'Saints and Heroes'?" *Irish Theological Quarterly* 59 (1993): 161–75. "The preferential option," Pope claims, "cannot be read accurately as a simple injunction to the wealthy to conform to the requirements of the just social order and sacrifice more of their resources for the sake of the poor. . . . [It] is intended to form the consciences of followers of Christ, not simply demand more giving; it functions to deepen and extend moral sensibilities beyond the conventional range of concern for the 'nearest and dearest.' . . . [It] targets not specific actions but the more basic motives and desires that underlie our behaviour" (172).
42 "Jesuits and the Situation of Women in Church and Civil Society," no. 9 (trans. *Origins* 24, no. 43 [April 13, 1995]: 741). Although the translation as reproduced in *Origins* is the final text, all of the congregation's texts are to be edited later for consistency of style and grammar.
43 See the article, primarily concerned with Latin America, by John F. Talbot, S.J., "Who Evangelizes Whom? The Poor Evangelizers," *Review for Religious,* November–December 1993, 893–97.
44 From the Puebla conference's "Preferential Option for the Poor" (no. 1147), quoted by Talbot, "Who Evangelizes Whom?" 894.
45 Quoted by Talbot, "Who Evangelizes Whom?" 896, from Sobrino's *Resurrección de la verdadera Iglesia,* 137–38.
46 Henri J. M. Nouwen and Walter J. Gaffney, *Aging* (Garden City, N.Y.: Doubleday Image Books, 1976), 101, 102.

4. Three Social Issues on an Upsurge

1 The Rothstein decision was reversed by a three-judge panel of the 9th Circuit Court of Appeals (filed March 9, 1995). In a two-to-one decision, Judge John Noonan wrote that the right to privacy may encompass freedom from unwanted medical intervention but not "the right to have a second person collaborate in your death." However, more recently the same 9th Circuit Court of Appeals, sitting en banc, struck down the earlier decision by an eight-to-three majority (filed March 6, 1996), holding "that a liberty interest exists in the choice of how and when one dies, and that the provision of the Washington statute banning assisted suicide, as applied to competent terminally ill adults who wish to hasten their deaths by obtaining medication prescribed by their doctors, violates the Due Process Clause."
2 Here I have been impressed and influenced by Charles Krauthammer's incisive

article "Judicially Assisted Suicide: This Is Not a Slippery Slope, It's a Cliff," *Washington Post,* May 13, 1994. This paragraph reflects my dependence on his insights.

3 Peter J. Bernardi, S.J., "The Hidden Engines of the Suicide Rights Movement," *America* 172, no. 16 (May 6, 1995): 14-17, at 16. The letter appeared in the September 14, 1993, edition of the *Press Democrat.* I am also indebted to Bernardi's article for the information on the Hogan, Rothstein, and Noonan legal decisions mentioned above.

4 See the Op-Ed piece by Lucette Lagnado, "Assisted Suicide and Rational Choice," *New York Times,* Aug. 4, 1995.

5 For an uncommonly open effort to explore ethical boundaries and distinctions, and to probe arguments both for and against changes in the law that would extend the range of individual choices regarding our dying, see the address given at Santa Clara University, May 1, 1995, by Margaret A. Farley, "Issues in Contemporary Christian Ethics: The Choice of Death in a Medical Context," published in the series The Santa Clara Lectures 1, no. 3 (1995).

6 Bernardi, "Hidden Engines," 16.

7 Karl Rahner, *Schriften zur Theologie* 15: *Wissenschaft und christlicher Glaube* (Zurich: Benziger, 1980), 20.

8 Karl Rahner, "Following the Crucified," *Theological Investigations* 18: *God and Revelation* (New York: Crossroad, 1983), 157-70, at 165-66. A major article on suffering and dying; to it I am deeply indebted, for my personal and professional life.

9 Ibid., 166, 167.

10 Ibid., 168.

11 Ibid., 158.

12 See ibid., 160-61.

13 The quotation is Rahner's vivid phrase, ibid., 169.

14 Margaret Dorgan, D.C.M., "A Spiritual Pragmatist and Suffering," *Living Pulpit* 4, no. 2 (April-June 1995): 18-19, at 18.

15 From a letter of July 15, 1995. Since these paragraphs of mine were composed, John Carmody has passed from us.

16 See the comments on this text, specifically on the meaning of *psyche,* by Joseph A. Fitzmyer, S.J., *The Gospel According to Luke (I-IX)* (Garden City, N.Y.: Doubleday, 1981), 788.

17 See Mary Catherine Hilkert, O.P., "Key Religious Symbols: Christ and God," *Theological Studies* 56 (1995): 341-52, at 344ff. Her article is part of a review of current literature on feminist theology.

18 I am quoting Pheme Perkins in her review of Schüssler Fiorenza's *Jesus, Miriam's Child, Sophia's Prophet: Critical Issues in Feminist Christology* (New York: Continuum, 1995) in *America* 172, no. 17 (May 13, 1995): 26-27, at 26.

19 Elizabeth A. Johnson, "Jesus and Salvation," *Proceedings of the Catholic Theological Society of America* 49 (1994): 1-18, at 15.

20 For details see my memorial homily for Father Arrupe, "Hands Nailed Down,"

in my collection *When Christ Meets Christ: Homilies on the Just Word* (New York: Paulist, 1993), 179–84. Arrupe was working as a Jesuit missionary in Hiroshima when the first atomic bomb fell on August 6, 1945.

21 For this overview I am deeply indebted to the Jesuit Richard Leonard's highly useful *Beloved Daughters: 100 Years of Papal Teaching on Women* (Melbourne, Australia: David Lovell, 1995), though I have made every effort to probe the most significant documents personally.

22 See Leo's 1891 encyclical *Rerum novarum (On the Condition of Labor)*, passim.

23 Pius XI, encyclical *Casti connubii (On Chaste Wedlock)*, 1930, section 74.

24 See the 1931 encyclical *Quadragesimo anno (Reconstruction of the Social Order)*, passim.

25 See, e.g., Pius XII's *Address to Women of "Catholic Action"* (Oct. 26, 1941), *Address to Newlyweds* (April 8, 1942), and *Address on Women's Duties in Social and Political Life* (Oct. 21, 1945).

26 In the context of "signs of the times," Vatican II's Pastoral Constitution on the Church in the Modern World (*Gaudium et spes*, 1965) recognizes the man/woman tensions and imbalances in the world. And among its closing messages, the council directly addresses women, proclaiming that "the hour is coming, in fact has come, when the vocation of woman is being achieved in its fullness, the hour in which woman acquires in the world an influence, an effect, and a power never hitherto achieved. . . . Women of the entire universe, whether Christian or non-believing, you to whom life is entrusted at this grave moment in history, it is for you to save the peace of the world" (trans. from *The Documents of Vatican II*, ed. Walter M. Abbott, S.J. [New York: Herder and Herder/Association Press, 1966], 733–74).

27 See *Inter insigniores*, section 5 (*Acta apostolicae sedis* 69 [1977]: 108–13).

28 Important evidence for papal understanding of woman's dignity is to be found in Mariological documents: e.g., Leo XIII's 1892 encyclical on the rosary, *Magnae Dei matris;* Pius X's 1904 encyclical on the Immaculate Conception, *Ad diem illum;* Pius XI's 1931 encyclical *Lux veritatis,* celebrating the fifteenth centenary of the Council of Ephesus; Pius XII's apostolic constitution *Munificentissimus Deus,* defining Mary's assumption into heaven in soul and body, and his insistence that Mary is a model for men as well as women; Paul VI's 1974 apostolic exhortation on devotion to Mary, *Marialis cultus,* placing Mary in a Christological context, declaring that Christ is the only way to the Father. John Paul II signals a fresh approach when he brings together Catholicism's Mariological traditions and the Church's social doctrine. See Leonard, *Beloved Daughters*, 30–34.

29 For *Mulieris dignitatem* I shall be using the Vatican's English-language text as reproduced in *Origins* 18 (1988): 261, 263–83.

30 *Mulieris dignitatem* I, 1 (*Origins*, 263); II, 6 (*Origins*, 265).

31 Ibid., III, 7 (*Origins*, 266, 267).

32 Ibid., III, 8 (*Origins*, 267).

33 Ibid., IV, 9 (*Origins*, 268). This, I discovered early in my study of the Church Fathers, is one (but not the only) patristic tradition; see my *The Image of God in*

Man According to Cyril of Alexandria (Washington, D.C.: Catholic University of America, 1957), 153-59.

34 *Mulieris dignitatem* IV, 10 (*Origins*, 269).

35 Ibid., IV, 11 (*Origins*, 270).

36 See the long section ibid., V, 12-16 (*Origins*, 270-73).

37 Ibid., V, 16 (*Origins*, 273).

38 Ibid., VII, 26 (*Origins*, 278-79).

39 *Ordinatio sacerdotalis*, no. 4; trans. from (London) *Tablet*, June 4, 1994, 720-21, at 721.

40 John Courtney Murray, S.J., *The Problem of God Yesterday and Today* (New Haven: Yale University Press, 1964), 44-45.

41 Pius XII, apostolic constitution *Munificentissimus Deus*, Nov. 1, 1950.

42 Illuminating discussions of pertinent issues can be found in Avery Dulles, *The Survival of Dogma* (Garden City, N.Y.: Doubleday, 1971). See, e.g., chapter 6, "Doctrinal Authority in the Church," 95-107, particularly his observations on the deterioration of a proper working relationship between bishops and theologians.

43 Francis Sullivan, S.J., "New Claims for the Pope," (London) *Tablet*, June 19, 1994, 767-69. Rome's official comment on the letter stated that the doctrine taught therein "always requires the full and unconditional assent of the faithful."

44 Quoted ibid., 768.

45 Ibid., 769.

46 Leonard, *Beloved Daughters*, 71.

47 As for an argument from Scripture, it is pertinent to observe that, in a report two decades ago, the Pontifical Biblical Commission concluded: "It does not seem that the New Testament by itself alone will permit us to settle in a clear way and once and for all the problem of the possible accession of women to the presbyterate." The commission noted that some do find in Scripture "sufficient indications to exclude this possibility," while others "wonder if the church hierarchy, entrusted with the sacramental economy, would be able to entrust the ministries of Eucharist and reconciliation to women in light of circumstances, without going against Christ's original intentions" (text under heading "Can Women Be Priests?" *Origins* 6, no. 6 [July 1, 1976]: 92-96, at 96, part 4, no. 2). The English translation was fashioned by *Origins* from the original French; the editors preface the translation by stating that "the members voted 12-5 that scriptural grounds alone are not enough to exclude the possibility of ordaining women" (92). They also note that the "report became public after a source unrelated to the commission made it available to the press" (92).

48 Raymond E. Brown, S.S., *Biblical Reflections on Crises Facing the Church* (New York: Paulist, 1975), 51; italics in text.

49 John Paul II, *Ordinatio sacerdotalis*, no. 4.

50 Vatican II, Declaration on Religious Freedom, no. 2.

51 Elisabeth Schüssler Fiorenza, "Feminist Theology as a Critical Theology of Liberation," *Theological Studies* 36 (1975): 605-26, at 611, quoting from Weil's *The Need for Roots* (New York, 1971), 225.

52 Ibid., 611, 620, 621.

53 Elisabeth Schüssler Fiorenza, *In Memory of Her: A Feminist Theological Reconstruction of Christian Origins* (New York: Crossroad, 1983), 24.

54 Leonard, *Beloved Daughters,* 84.

55 Worth noting here are three ecclesiologies within Roman Catholicism; for, as Raymond Brown believes, "the ecclesiology that dominates may well tip the scales for or against ordaining women." Blueprint ecclesiology presupposes a God-given blueprint in which all the basic structures were mapped out; ordination of women was not included. Erector-set ecclesiology claims that Christians are free to build the Church as utility directs; if the Church needs women priests, who is to say no? In-between ecclesiology combines the better elements of the other two: neither a blueprint nor an "anything useful" mentality; rather, a set of instructions together with the will of Christ and the guidance of the Spirit. Brown distinguishes the three as respectively "the firm, the free, and the fickle." See Brown, *Biblical Reflections,* 50-61.

56 Edward J. Kilmartin, S.J., "Apostolic Office: Sacrament of Christ," *Theological Studies* 36 (1975): 243-64, at 263.

57 Dennis Michael Ferrara, "Representation or Self-Effacement? The Axiom *in persona Christi* in St. Thomas and the Magisterium," *Theological Studies* 55 (1994): 195-224. It is important to note that Ferrara, in a note (91, p. 224) on the "can" in the final sentence, insists that his sole competence in this article is "to remove the doctrinal objection against the Church's ordination of women and thereby move the question from the doctrinal to the prudential sphere" — practical questions on "should" rather than "can": e.g., ecumenical relations, geographical and cultural areas, church finances, etc.

58 Dennis Michael Ferrara, "The Ordination of Women: Tradition and Meaning," *Theological Studies* 55 (1994): 706-19.

59 Sara Butler, M.S.B.T., " *'In persona Christi'*: A Response to Dennis M. Ferrara," *Theological Studies* 56 (1995): 61-80, at 69, 80. Ferrara has responded to Butler's response, "A Reply to Sara Butler," *Theological Studies* 56 (1995): 81-91. He does dispute her individual charges but is convinced that what emerges overall "is a fundamental difference in theological mentality" (81).

60 English text reproduced from *Origins* 25, no. 24 (Nov. 30, 1995): 401, 403. Released with this response and translated in the same issue of *Origins* (403-5) were certain "Vatican Reflections on the Teaching of *Ordinatio sacerdotalis*." Among much else, these reflections note "the essential interdependence of holy Scripture and tradition," with the magisterium "an integral part of the tradition and . . . entrusted with the authentic interpretation of the word of God, written and handed down. . . . In the specific case of priestly ordination, the successors of the apostles have always observed the norm of conferring it only on men, and the magisterium, assisted by the Holy Spirit, teaches us that this did not occur by chance, habitual repetition, subjection to sociological conditioning, or even less because of some imaginary inferiority of women," but because the Church sees as a perennial norm the Lord's way of acting in choosing the Twelve (404-

5). The reflections explicitly deny that "the exclusion of women from the priestly ministry represents a form of injustice or discrimination" and offers as proof the example of the Virgin Mary, neither apostle nor ministerial priest (404).

61 Ladislas Orsy, S.J., "The Congregation's 'Response': Its Authority and Meaning," *America* 171, no. 19 (Dec. 9, 1995): 4-5.

62 Ibid.

63 Ibid. I should note that an official of the congregation, who asked not to be named but spoke on behalf of the congregation's secretary, Archbishop Tarcisio Bertone, "disputed Father Orsy's interpretation that the congregation's text tries to give more weight to the teaching than the original papal letter" (*Catholic News Service*, Dec. 1, 1995).

64 Francis A. Sullivan, S.J., "Guideposts from Catholic Tradition," *America* 171, no. 19 (Dec. 9, 1995): 5-6, at 6. In response to Sullivan, the same congregation official quoted in the previous note stated that the idea that "the ordinary universal magisterium should be subject to a universal consultation of the episcopate is not found in the Code of Canon Law or in the practice of the Church." The pope "is not obliged" to consult with the world's bishops on any issue (*Catholic News Service*, Dec. 1, 1995). The response misses Sullivan's crucial point: how does the pope know that the type of consensus required for an infallible teaching of the ordinary magisterium actually exists?

65 A chronic thorn in Rome's theological flesh, Hans Küng, the well-known professor of ecumenical theology and director of the Institute for Ecumenical Research at the University of Tübingen, is convinced that the CDF document confronts Catholic theologians "with a dilemma that they can only avoid against their better judgment: Either they accept the 'infallible' doctrine of the ordinary and universal magisterium, in which case they must advocate the impossibility of the ordination of women and much else with 'full, definitive, and thus irrevocable assent' and must join with the pope in saying that women are excluded from the priesthood now and forever; or they advocate the possibility of women being ordained, with good theological reasons for doing so—but in this case they are obliged with all due decorum to call the infallibility of the church's teaching authority into question." He believes that only a third Vatican Council "would release Catholic theology from the dilemma in which it finds itself at present" ("Theologians Now Face Either-Or Situation," *National Catholic Reporter* 32, no. 8 [Dec. 15, 1995]: 6-7, at 7).

66 Avery Dulles, S. J., "Gender and Priesthood: Examining the Teaching," *Origins* 25, no. 45 (May 2, 1996) 778-84.

67 The official English version was published by the Vatican Polyglot Press in 1986.

68 *Pastoral Care*, no. 5, par. 2. For an earlier pronouncement, see the Congregation's *Declaration on Certain Questions concerning Social Ethics (Persona humana)*, Dec. 29, 1975.

69 See, e.g., Gerald D. Coleman, S.S., "The Vatican Statement on Homosexuality," *Theological Studies* 48 (1987): 726-34, specifically 728-31, a brief but pungent evaluation of Old and New Testament "antihomosexual references": "In all

probability, the biblical writers in each instance were speaking of homosexual acts undertaken by persons whom the authors presumed to be heterosexually constituted. Each biblical reference to homosexual activity, then, must be interpreted against this presumption" (729-30).

70 *Pastoral Care,* no. 6, par. 1.

71 See, e.g., *Persona humana,* no. 8.

72 *Pastoral Care,* no. 7, pars. 1 and 2. Unfortunately, the letter concludes its treatment of homosexual acts by speaking of "a disordered inclination which is essentially self-indulgent" (no. 7, par. 2). The fact that the immediately preceding clause had expressly stated that gay persons are "often generous and giving of themselves" has persuaded at least one Catholic scholar to infer that the charge of self-indulgence refers "essentially to the preference of one's homosexual proclivity over God's creative design, and not necessarily to the more basely selfish motive of satisfying one's physical passion" (Bruce Williams, O.P., "Homosexuality: The New Vatican Statement," *Theological Studies* 48 [1987]: 259-77, at 262-63).

73 *Pastoral Care,* no. 3, par. 2.

74 Ibid., no. 3, pars. 2 and 3.

75 Ibid., no. 2, par. 1; no. 16.

76 Coleman, "Vatican Statement on Homosexuality," 734.

77 On AIDS, see *Pastoral Care,* no. 9, pars. 2 and 3: "Even when the practice of homosexuality may seriously threaten the lives and well-being of a large number of people, its advocates remain undeterred and refuse to consider the magnitude of the risks involved. The Church can never be so callous." On other specified issues see ibid., no. 17, par. 9; no. 10, par. 2; no. 10, par. 2.

78 Ibid., no. 10, par. 1.

79 Ibid., no. 15, par. 3.

80 For detailed documentation see the valuable volume edited by Jeannine Gramick and Robert Nugent, *Voices of Hope: A Collection of Positive Catholic Writings on Gay and Lesbian Issues* (New York: Center for Homophobia Education, 1995).

81 *Some Considerations,* Foreword and nos. 11 and 12. It is only fair to point out, as Vatican spokesman Joaquin Navarro-Vals did, that the document was "not intended to be an official and public instruction . . . but a background resource offering discreet assistance to those who may be confronted with the task of evaluating draft legislation regarding non-discrimination on the basis of sexual orientation."

82 For a large selection of such responses, see Gramick and Nugent, *Voices of Hope,* 178-224.

83 Vincent J. Genovesi, S.J., "Human and Civil Rights for Gays and Lesbians," *America* 172, no. 14 (April 22, 1995): 15-20, at 17. John F. Tuohey, assistant professor of moral theology at the Catholic University of America, in an article entitled "The C.D.F. and Homosexuals: Rewriting the Moral Tradition," *America* 167, no. 6 (Sept. 12, 1992): 136-38, has claimed that, at least on the issue of homosexuality, the Congregation appears to be saying that the end justifies the

means. "With casuistry, the tradition can tolerate some *indirect* discrimination. However, and this is critically important, it can do so only when there is a proportionate reason to justify the evil. The C.D.F., in contrast to this tradition, not only calls for *direct* discrimination, it does so without presenting any proportionate reason that might justify it" (136).

84 Russell Connors, column in Cleveland's *Catholic Universe Bulletin,* Aug. 28, 1992, reproduced in Gramick and Nugent, *Voices of Hope,* 202–4.

85 Genovesi, "Human and Civil Rights," 19.

86 So Richard L. Smith, "Gays and the Bishops: Searching for Common Ground," *America* 171, no. 8 (Sept. 24, 1994): 12–17.

87 Ibid., 17.

88 See David E. DeCosse, "The Catholic Case for Inclusion," *America* 168, no. 16 (May 8, 1993): 15–16, for a persuasive argument that the Ancient Order of Hibernians would have affirmed the Catholic "exuberant affirmation of life" and might have reminded "a broken city for a few moments of the possibility of a common life" had it not excluded the Irish Lesbian and Gay Organization from the St. Patrick's Day Parade in New York City.

89 " 'I'm Here': An Interview with Andrew Sullivan," *America* 168, no. 16 (May 8, 1993): 5–11.

90 Ibid. In fairness, it must be recognized that in a number of Catholic dioceses the spiritual care of gays and lesbians is a significant ministry; I experienced one such ministry in the Archdiocese of Los Angeles.

91 Quoted by Paul Giurlanda, "What about Our Church's Children?" *America* 168, no. 16 (May 8, 1993): 12–14, at 12.

92 John Courtney Murray, S.J., "Freedom, Authority, Community," *America* 115 (1966): 734–41, at 735. For details on the "old look" and the new vision, see my essay "The Authority Crisis in Catholicism: Analysis and Prognosis," in *Hope: Psychiatry's Commitment,* Papers Presented to Leo H. Bartemeier, M.D., on the Occasion of His 75th Birthday, ed. A. W. R. Sipe (New York: Brunner/Mazel, 1970), 203–14.

93 Quotation from Second Vatican Council, Declaration on Religious Freedom, no. 1.

94 Murray, "Freedom, Authority, Community," 736.

95 William J. O'Malley, S.J., "The Goldilocks Method," *America* 165, no. 14 (Nov. 9, 1991): 334–39, at 336.

96 For the text see my collection *Still Proclaiming Your Wonders: Homilies for the Eighties* (New York: Paulist, 1984), 25–30.

97 The whole is reproduced in *Preaching: The Art and the Craft* (New York: Paulist, 1987), 68–77, quotations at 76, 77.

Index